A HOUSE IN THE CITY

H. Dickson McKenna

A HOUSE IN THE CITY

A GUIDE TO BUYING AND RENOVATING OLD ROW HOUSES

VNR VAN NOSTRAND REINHOLD COMPANY
NEW YORK   CINCINNATI   TORONTO   LONDON   MELBOURNE

Van Nostrand Reinhold Company Regional Offices:
New York Cincinnati Chicago Millbrae Dallas
Van Nostrand Reinhold Company International Offices:
London Toronto Melbourne

Designed by Jean Callan King
Printed by Halliday Lithograph Corporation

Published by Van Nostrand Reinhold Company,
450 West 33rd Street, New York, N.Y. 10001.
Published simultaneously in Canada by
Van Nostrand Reinhold Ltd.

2 4 6 8 10 12 14 16 15 13 11 9 7 5 3 1

PHOTOGRAPHY CREDITS

Kingsley Carrington Fairbridge: pp. 8, 9, 11, 21, 23, 26, 27, 32, 34, 37, 41, 42 (lower), 50, 51 (left), 56, 57, 64 (top), 72, 74, 75, 76, 77, 78, 80, 90, 91, 98, 104, 105, 122, 124/Jack Pickens Coble: p. 13/Daniel Hirsch: p. 15/New York Historical Society, New York City: pp. 17, 18 (lower), 19, 20 (lower)/Long Island Historical Society: p. 18 (upper)/Avery Library, Columbia University: pp. 20 (upper), 22, 33 (right), 42 (upper), 93, 108, 109/Jean Callan King: pp. 25, 30, 31, 35, 36 (lower), 40, 43, 44, 46, 47, 48 (upper), 49, 51 (right), 94, 96, 99 (upper), 100, 101, 132/National Trust for Historic Preservation: Row Houses, Inc., p. 28/Earnest Burden: pp. 39, 45, 120, 121/Frank Lotz Miller: p. 54/George Cserna: pp. 58, 59/New Haven Redevelopment Agency: p. 70/Bill Maris: pp. 126, 127/Jane Rady: pp. 128, 129/Larry Mersel: pp. 134, 135/John Veltri: p. 141/Charles Burck: pp. 151, 152, 153/Tomas Breuer: pp. 152-157/Author: pp. 31, 33 (left), 48 (lower), 60, 64 (left), 65, 66, 84, 85, 89, 99 (lower), 118, 119, 123, 125, 139.

ARCHITECTURE CREDITS

Gruzen & Partners, AIA: p. 15/Jack Pickens Coble, AIA: p. 26/Henry G. Grimball, AIA: p. 54/John Lloyd: p. 71/Copelin & Lee, AIA: pp. 119 (upper), 125 (lower), 150/Earnest Burden, AIA: pp. 120, 121/R & J Newman: pp. 126, 127/James Byron Bell, AIA: pp. 128, 129/Peter Phillips, AIA, James Dixon, Designer: pp. 134, 135/Richard W. Snibbe, FAIA, paintings by Theo Hios: pp. 139-143/Michael Lax, Designer: pp. 144, 145/Jan Hird Pokorny, FAIA: pp. 146-149/Stanley Maurer, AIA, and Laurie Maurer, AIA: pp. 152-157.

DRAWINGS

All the pen-and-ink sketches are by Jane George. Most of the architectural plans and sections were drawn by Spencer George.

To the memory of my grandfather
Walter Dickson, FAIA
and to my parents

CONTENTS

INTRODUCTION

This is a book about finding, evaluating, buying, renovating, and living in city houses. The usual city house is a row house: it can be anywhere from two to five stories high, is built of brownstone, limestone, brick, or wood, occupies a narrow, rectangular plot of land, and shares side walls with its neighbors. In certain areas such a house can cost half a million dollars, or even two million dollars. A great many are available in the range between twenty thousand and fifty thousand dollars. A few are much cheaper.

The row house now available at a reasonable price was probably constructed at least seventy years ago. It was originally occupied by a moderately prosperous family, but its neighborhood has deteriorated in the last few decades, and perhaps for many years it has been a rooming house. On the surface it is battered and worn. But it can once again become a handsome and comfortable home—in a clean and safe neighborhood.

In recent years a large number of old city houses have been purchased and renovated by people one might expect to find in suburban homes or middle-income apartments. And that is where they come from. For a variety of reasons—for the apartment dweller, perhaps the desire to own the place one lives in and to have a garden and play area; for the suburbanite, perhaps the desire to be close to work and to city life—they have forsaken commuter train or cramped apartment and committed themselves to the city house. They now occupy thousands of row houses in the nation's cities, and some enterprising individuals have made homes of carriage houses, churches, firehouses, banks, and even abandoned gas stations. Like all home buyers, they have been motivated mainly by self-interest, but the cities they live in have benefited too as block after block of deteriorating buildings has been revitalized.

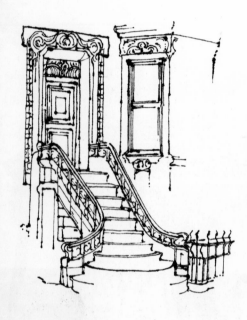

A growing interest in the city house is apparent. Magazines that were once totally concerned with suburban "homemaking" have devoted entire issues to the city house. Articles on financing, evaluating, and renovating city houses appear frequently in newspapers and general-circulation magazines, and there are local publications, such as *The Brownstoner* of New York City's Brownstone Revival Committee, aimed specifically at city homeowners. Neighborhood associations, made up primarily of city homeowners, flourish. Programs and legislation on the federal, state, and municipal levels encourage the rehabilitation of city houses. Massive urban-renewal programs, federally funded, offer financial aid to city homeowners.

New York City's new Master Plan is a good example of official interest in the renovation of houses. As the Master Plan explains the phenomenon: "One of the most encouraging things that is happening in this city is the way citizens are reviving neighborhoods on their own. Of their own free will, in the face of considerable odds and dire predictions, a growing number of younger people have been expending great amounts of psychic energy and borrowed money on the purchase and remodeling of old brownstones in beat-up neighborhoods. The people are of all kinds—artists, writers, professionals, junior executives, civil servants, returned suburbanites. What binds them is a dogged common sense. They like the city and in their old brownstones they have found a way to live in spaciousness and style at reasonable cost, close to their jobs, and close to challenge."

Nevertheless, for every couple who actually purchase a row house, there are probably a dozen who are attracted by the idea but are afraid that it may be too much for them. This book is for those people. In it I have tried to point out some of the problems involved in finding, buying, renovating, and living in a city house, and to present ways in which these problems can be solved or avoided.

As an architect and the owner of a city house I am first to admit that this book is not all-inclusive; it could not possibly be. Two city houses side by side may look the same, but each has an identity all its own, and each will present its special problems and charms to the buyer. Two city houses in different cities will be more obviously different; zoning, financing, construction codes, and every other factor will vary somewhat from city to city. Since I live and work in New York City—my own house is in one of Brooklyn's row-house neighborhoods—New York is the city I know best, but whenever possible I have tried to include information about houses in other urban centers too. I have confined myself, for the most part, to the row house, since it is what the prospective homeowner will find available—and, like the interest in renovation, it is a nationwide phenomenon.

ONE | A HISTORY OF THE ROW HOUSE

In cities and towns throughout history the row house has been more common than the detached or free-standing house, simply because it has always been a practical shelter for the lower and middle classes. It is efficient to construct, is relatively easy to heat, and requires only a small plot of land. Officials and nobility lived in detached houses, but the majority of city dwellers lived in row houses. In Kahun, Egypt, a town built about 2670 B.C., row houses were used to house workmen during the construction of the Illahun pyramid for Usertesen II. In the fourth century B.C. the Greeks were building row houses. By the eleventh century A.D. many European cities contained rows of two- and three-story houses encircling gardens and courts.

The row house as we know it, however, began to appear shortly after the London fire of 1666. Before the fire London had been expanding in a rapid, haphazard fashion, with street construction following the meandering paths of cattle drovers. Like the Chicago fire two centuries later, the London blaze leveled great portions of the city. Since the destruction forced Londoners to rebuild from the ground up, it made real city planning possible, and it also stimulated legislation that encouraged row-house construction.

The row houses built in London after the fire were not merely attached structures sharing party walls. They were uniform houses erected by the same builder, from the same plans, at the same time. As a result, their attached facades dis-

The Royal Crescent in Bath, England—built in the eighteenth century and still one of the best examples of unified streetscape planning. Modern planners are both consciously and unconsciously influenced by its design, as can be seen in the plans and model on the next page, which are of a proposed development in Paerdegat, Brooklyn. In the plan, a series of ellipses enclose open spaces. Each house contains two duplexes.

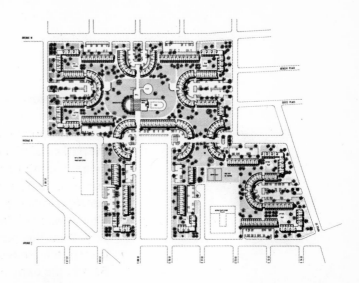

15

played a harmony of design formerly seen only in palaces, churches, and large public buildings.

For obvious reasons of economy, they were narrow at the front and as long as the particular block would permit—usually thirty-five to fifty feet. The kitchen was located in the basement, and coal was stored under the sidewalk. Each floor contained a front and a back room and often a small room or closet in the rear. A staircase ran up one side, and servants' rooms were located on the top floor or attic. It was an efficient use of space—and it still is.

Perhaps the most remarkable achievement in English row-house design, one that still influences architects both in Europe and America, began in the town of Bath in the early eighteenth century. Thought to have health-restoring waters, Bath was changing at this period from a quiet town to a flourishing resort. In the summers London society flocked to Bath, and the town soon began to mushroom. To deal with this sudden expansion, Bath employed the architect and builder John Wood to plot the course of the town's growth.

Wood drew up the first plans in 1725. From the beginning he hoped to give the town a flavor of ancient Rome. In 1754, under his direction, work began on the Circus, thirty-three elegant row houses enclosing an enormous garden. Wood died during the construction of the Circus, but the work was completed by his son, John Wood II.

After finishing the Circus, the younger Wood began work on an even grander project, the Royal Crescent. A semi-elliptical block overlooking a spacious lawn, the Royal Crescent consisted of thirty row houses with facades of Ionic columns. Many architects today consider the Circus and the Royal Crescent to be the finest extant examples of eighteenth-century row-house design. In fact it has influenced the most contemporary architects, as can be seen in the housing scheme shown on the preceding page.

THE ROW HOUSE IN AMERICA

Philadelphia was probably the first American city to adopt the English row house. By 1700, brick houses similar to those built in London after the fire were common in the city. The rise of land values and the gridiron plan of street layout devised by the surveyor Thomas Holme led to thin, rectangular lots, and soon the brick row house replaced the free-standing structure. Today these brick row houses are perhaps the most charming feature of the city.

Boston's first row houses were designed and erected in 1793-94 by the famous architect Charles Bulfinch. Bulfinch had visited London and Bath in 1787 and had greatly admired their elegant row houses. Remembering Bath's Royal Crescent, he designed the Tontine Crescent on Boston's South Side and later the Crescent on what is now Franklin Street. From 1832 to 1840, contractors erecting groups of ten or twelve houses from identical plans and elevations covered Boston's South Side with row houses. In recent years this and other Boston neighborhoods have undergone massive renewal, but many row houses remain and are now being successfully restored.

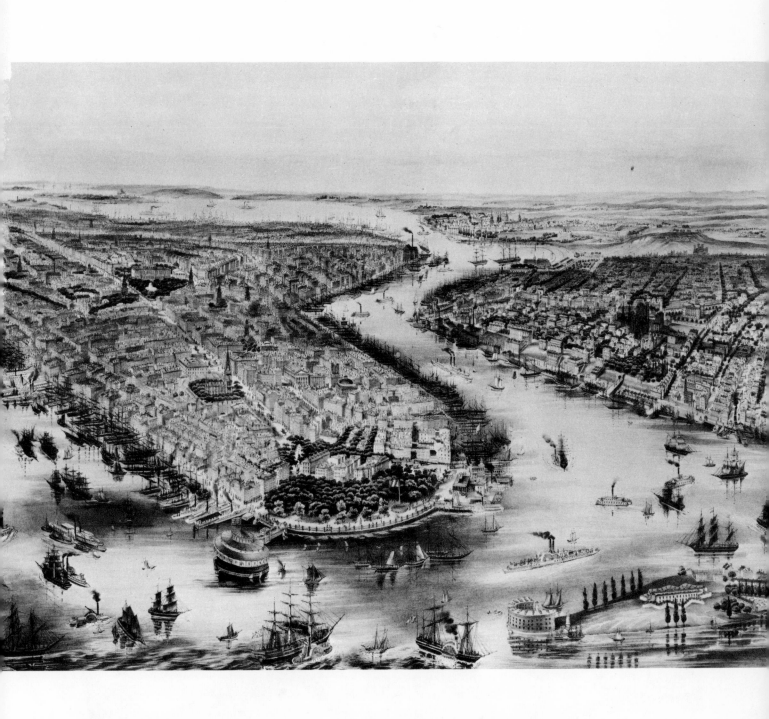

A somewhat compressed view of the lower end of Manhattan and the Brooklyn
shore, drawn about the middle of the nineteenth century. Trinity Church, prominent
in downtown Manhattan, was the first important brownstone building in New York.

This drawing of a corner in downtown Brooklyn, done in the first half of the nineteenth century, shows brick, brownstone, and wood row houses. This corner is now part of the site of the Brooklyn Civic Center.

Notice how the prototypical grid plan prepared for Manhattan by a surveyor in 1811 ignored topography, represented by the crude contour lines. Central Park was a later addition.

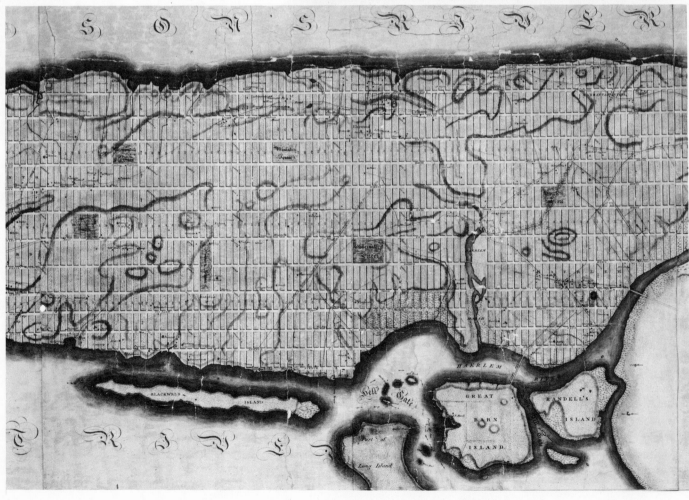

The beginnings of a city block, in a photograph of 1887. These houses, built in groups by contractors, were waiting to be bought by speculators; soon more rows of houses filled in the gaps.

Row-house construction in New York City began during the Federal period, about 1820 to 1830. In Greenwich Village there are still several row houses constructed during this period in the best Federal style. Early New York row houses followed the London plan with a few variations—most notably, the stoop. In the London plan, the only front entrance was at street level, leading to the dining room. New York designers, influenced by the houses built by early Dutch settlers, added a stoop, or exterior flight of stairs leading to the parlor floor, thus adding a second front entrance to the house.

One of the major reasons for the popularity of row-house construction in New York in the early years of the nineteenth century was the gridiron plan adopted by the city in 1811 during the administration of Mayor DeWitt Clinton. The uniform, rectangular plan for street layout—which later caused the novelist Edith Wharton to refer to New York as "this cramped horizontal gridiron of a town"—was strongly attacked by many New York residents when it was introduced. It was claimed that the plan called for a city with a population greater than any "this side of China." The city commissioners defended the gridiron plan heartily, holding that it was entirely possible that in a hundred years or so New York would be quite heavily settled.

Blocks of houses like these shown in an architect's
sketch were built by speculator landowners
and then sold off one by one for a handsome profit.

New Yorkers serenade Governor Tilden at his
Gramercy Park house in a contemporary steel
engraving.

New York was not the originator of the gridiron plan, but was certainly unusually persistent in following it. Philadelphia, for example, had earlier adopted a gridiron, but had provided for parks and open spaces. In New York there were no such provisions. Only later were such open spaces as Central Park incorporated. Luckily, some parts of New York, such as lower Manhattan, were not affected by the grid pattern. In Greenwich Village there are still curving streets, angled to follow old property lines that predate the establishment of the gridiron plan.

One surprising result of the gridiron plan was a variety in architectural detail. As speculators erected row houses by the thousand, filling virtually identical rectangular plots on virtually identical blocks, the competition to achieve originality in design became extremely keen. Glamorous facades and fantastic variations of Moorish, Spanish Renaissance, and English Tudor architecture flourished for a few blocks and were never seen again. Other variations, such as bay windows, caught on everywhere in the city.

Rows and rows of houses like these were built in the late nineteenth century for families of moderate income. Standardized lintels, sills, and other items were used to reduce costs. Ornament was usually stamped galvanized metal. These facades are the typical pattern.

Two of the many variations developed later in the nineteenth century. Each of these houses was built on the last remaining lot between rows of existing houses, and each was built for an individual client—who expressed his individuality.

Built at the same time by the same builder, this row of two-story-and-basement houses displays the best of the American nineteenth-century streetscape. Only one retains the original ironwork.

THE TYPICAL NINETEENTH-CENTURY HOUSE

One of the most prolific designers working during the early years of New York row-house construction was Calvin Pollard, an architect and surveyor who maintained New York offices from 1830 to 1858. Anyone who has ever been inside a New York row house is familiar with his standard layout.

Under the high stoop was a servants' entrance to the ground floor. The ground floor contained either a servants' parlor or a dining room in front, and a large kitchen in the back, which opened onto a yard used to dry laundry and sometimes to store wood and coal. If the dining room was on the ground floor, it was separated from the kitchen by a pantry with a sliding-door passthrough. If the dining room was on the floor above, food was sent up in a dumbwaiter—a device that accounted for much of the comfort of row-house living—and the entire ground floor was relegated to servants and services.

An interesting architectural feature of the typical row-house kitchen was the stove niche, formed by the masonry supports for the hearth in the room above. The kitchen ceiling was low, so it was not desirable to support this hearth with projecting corbels. The coal stove fit neatly between the masonry supports and vented into the chimney flue—usually around the clock; it was banked at night, then opened up in the morning to prepare breakfast.

Lavatories with marble counters, and often with brass fixtures, are still found in some houses and are treasured by their owners. Reproductions are now available.

The first, or parlor, floor consisted of a hallway and invariably two parlors, separated by sliding doors and usually equipped with identical fireplaces and mantels. On the next floor were a front bedroom, a back bedroom, two large closets, and a primitive bath at the end of the hall. The front bedroom was usually L-shaped, running the entire width of the house at the extreme front. Thus there was an alcove at the front for a bed, leaving a large rectangular area that could serve as a sitting room. Between the front bedroom and the back bedroom was a passageway that was the forerunner of the modern dressing room. It contained a sink and a cupboard for each bedroom. The row-house buyer who is lucky enough to find these central sinks—usually marble—in good repair would be wise to think twice before ripping them out in favor of more closet space or a windowless bathroom. The cabinet and drawers may be fine old wood, and the little sink areas could turn out to be one of the most charming features of the house. Also, when the passage is left open, the entire floor can be cross-ventilated.

The top floor followed the pattern of the floor below, except that the front room was square, since there was no ascending staircase. Also, instead of a bathroom at the end of the hall, there was often a small third bedroom.

Usually all the windows facing the street were fitted with interior shutters. (Often there were exterior shutters on the back windows, with ingenious hardware to hold them in place when open.) The set of shutters for each window had eight panels—that is, two pairs of folding shutters—and they folded back neatly into the niches at each side of the window. Some of the panels had fixed or movable louvers. Fortunately, many rooming-house landlords who have not wanted to bother painting or repairing shutters have merely nailed them back into their niches, and so they have survived. They may be somewhat the worse for wear and will almost certainly have many coats of paint that must be removed, but they are worth the trouble. New shutters can be bought, but they will be quite expensive and not as well made as the old ones. Perhaps you think you do not want shutters, but if the house you buy has them, try living with them awhile. They are a pleasant architectural element in any room, they give a sense of security and privacy, and they provide excellent light control.

On this page, a contemporary emulation of Gramercy Park's nineteenth-century ironwork. The simplified, elegant design relates an otherwise plain building to its neighbors. The construction drawing was just one of many required—by city authorities as well as by the ironworker. On the next page, an original ironwork facade, also in Gramercy Park, and some details of cast-iron railings. Nineteenth-century builders' catalogs listed hundreds of different patterns and shapes.

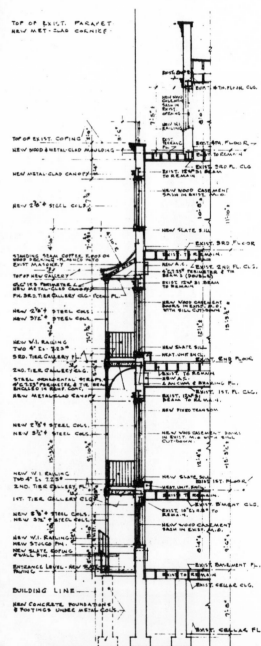

Row House (1840) in Hallowell, Maine.

ROW HOUSES IN MILL TOWNS

As the nineteenth century wore on, row-house construction moved west from New York to Pittsburgh and Chicago and finally to San Francisco, where handsome wooden rows covered the steep hills. The row house also moved north, to the mill towns of New England. Along with the large stone and/or brick industrial buildings built during the early industrial revolution there were fine examples of row houses erected to house the mill-workers. Textile mills four and five stories high were built of fire-resistant materials—brick walls with heavy timber columns and thick plank flooring, a system which became known as "mill construction."

Rows of two-story buildings were built to house the workers, who usually had large families (child labor had not yet come into disfavor). Most of these have long since disappeared, but a group of five living units at Hallowell, Maine, has been reclaimed and offered as a condominium. Built in 1840, the row is structurally sound and attractive in its proportions, and contains all the original window sashes, chimneys, and fireplaces.

THE ROW HOUSE IN THE TWENTIETH CENTURY

Early in this century, row-house construction waned. The single exception was Philadelphia, where there was massive row-house construction to house low-income families. In most other American cities, however, multiple dwellings became the rule—tenements for the working classes and apartment houses for those who could afford them. Also during this time the great exodus from the cities began—to garden apartments and small detached houses in the suburbs. Until a few years ago almost all urban and suburban residential construction seemed to fall into two distinct categories, the large apartment building and the sprawling development project of identical free-standing houses.

In the past few years, however, there have been signs that row-house construction may be coming back. In the suburbs many builders are now erecting what have come to be called "cluster houses." These are houses with common party walls, built more or less on open ground but with common utilities. It is interesting that these new row houses have the same basic layout and seem to appeal to the same type of family as those of the nineteenth century.

The advent of new building technology may also lead to more row-house construction. Already some architects are proposing construction of modular row houses as one solution to urban housing problems. Under this plan a family could buy a floor-through row-house module at a fairly low cost. Other modules could later be stacked on top of the original module when the family could afford to enlarge their house.

BUILDING MATERIALS

The first row houses in America were built of brick, much of it brought in as ballast on Dutch and English ships. Brick houses appeared in Philadelphia around 1700, and brick was the prime building material for row houses for nearly a century and a half.

Around 1840, however, there was a revival of Gothic architectural design in America, and stone replaced brick in many of the nation's public buildings and row houses. The most popular was brownstone, a close-grained, soft sandstone stained an even reddish-brown by traces of iron ore. It became so popular that today the word "brownstone" is often used to mean any nineteenth-century row house, even those with brick or limestone facades.

Many row houses were wood-frame and shingle, but few remain because they are vulnerable to fire. This one is typical, and still a handsome house, but unfortunately its neighbor has been ''improved.''

The use of brownstone began in New York and quickly spread across the country. You can find genuine ''brownstones'' on Commonwealth and Huntington Avenues in Boston, and on lakefront stretches in Chicago. Philadelphia, however, had quarries and clay pits nearby and was one of the few American cities where brownstone did not replace the traditional brick.

Although New York City is built on rock, it is a mica-flecked stone not suited to building. The rock of the Palisades, across the Hudson, was useful only as gravel. As a result, building stone had to be imported into the city. One source of New York's brownstone lies in a sandstone bed, twenty miles wide and a hundred miles long, that begins about sixty miles north of the city where the Connecticut River empties into Long Island Sound. The sandstone was quarried with a steam-driven channeling saw (invented about the middle of the nineteenth century) and transported down the river by barge. About the same distance from New York and west into New Jersey there was another sandstone bed, which was of equal importance as a source for the city's brownstone.

At first brownstone was used as a complete building material, wall-bearing and strong. It was relatively inexpensive, and if properly laid and cut cross-grain, it was extremely durable and would not flake. As the stone became more popular, however, builders began to use it as a facing over brick, and it was cut into thinner and thinner sections. The typical brownstone front today is therefore an unhappy sight—the thin slabs have chipped and flaked, sometimes beyond reclamation.

Wood was extensively used in the early years of row-house construction, but a great many wooden houses have since been destroyed by fire. The wood houses that remain, although they may appear dilapidated, are for the most part sturdy, durable structures. Most wood row houses were built with post-and-beam construction, the walls filled with masonry. Clapboards or shingles were then attached to the exterior. Although wood row houses are relatively scarce in eastern cities, they are plentiful in San Francisco, since the upper west coast has little stone, and wood is the prime building material.

STYLES

The remainder of this chapter is composed of brief descriptions of the most prominent of the various architectural styles of the row house. All row-house facades have much in common, but there are variations in windows, cornices, and doorways, and this makes it possible to identify most row houses as belonging to a particular era and exemplifying a particular style. However, such identifications are often very arbitrary, and some of the style classifications commonly used are quite artificial. Few houses are a pure expression of a particular style—for that matter, few styles are pure. I have used the standard style vocabulary in picture captions and elsewhere when it was desirable to identify a particular detail or to classify a particular building, and below I have

The Federal style. The 25-foot-wide house shown at left was built in the 1850's in what is now downtown Brooklyn. It was one of the first houses outside Brooklyn Heights to be renovated. The front doors have been stripped to natural wood and varnished. The doorway below is readily distinguished as Federal by its use of classical detail; note the complete columns set on either side of the wide center door.

tried to typify the different styles, but nevertheless the reader should remember that at least for nineteenth-century residential architecture, nomenclature is little more than a game.

FEDERAL (1820-1835)

The Federal style became prominent in American architecture soon after the revolution. It formed a bridge between the architecture of the colonial period and the Revival styles that began to appear in the 1830s.

Federal houses were usually built of brick, frequently laid in Flemish bond (the long and short sides of the bricks are laid alternately). The entrance to the parlor floor is flush with the facade and the stoop is low, usually made of brownstone. Some Federal houses also have a horsewalk, a narrow entry at street level which served as a passageway to stables in the rear.

Doors in Federal houses usually have six or eight panels. Windows are double-hung with six-over-six sash. Other characteristic features are arched windows, fan doorways, carved sunbursts, floral motifs set in exterior lintels and exterior walls at the basement level, dentils, cornices, entablatures, and wrought-iron railings, decorated with rosettes and pine-cone or pineapple finials. More elaborate Federal houses display fluted columns with Doric or Ionic capitals.

The Greek Revival style. The severe entablature, relying on proportion rather than embellishment for its effect, is characteristic.

GREEK REVIVAL (1834-1860)

The Greek Revival style, extremely evident in such neighborhoods as New York's Brooklyn Heights, supplanted the Federal style in row-house design. Borrowed from Roman and Egyptian designs as well as from the architecture of ancient Greece, it was a heavier, more masculine style than the Federal. In Greek Revival houses the detailed carvings around doorways and fireplaces common to the Federal style were replaced by wide, flat moldings or heavy, plain pilasters. This was in part because much of the work formerly done by hand was now done by steam-driven machinery. This new machinery also allowed the architect to design decorative details as well as the overall plans for the building.

The Greek Revival style introduced a sense of interior spaciousness. Ceilings were higher than in Federal houses, and the twin parlors on the main floor were separated by wide sliding doors, which could be opened to form a single room. Outside, fences were often decorated with frets, meanders, floral forms, cones, or anthemions.

The style originated in America and spread throughout the country. By the middle of the nineteenth century it was virtually the national architectural style.

GOTHIC REVIVAL (1844-1865)

The Gothic Revival style began to flourish in America about the same time as the Greek Revival, although to a lesser extent. One of the first architects to import this style was Benjamin Henry Latrobe, who employed the style in a country villa called Sedgeley, built in 1799 in what is now Philadelphia's Fairmont Park.

Sometimes called the Christian style, Gothic Revival was seen primarily in churches, especially in England, where it was encouraged by the British Church Building Acts passed by Parliament during the early nineteenth century. Descriptions of houses built in this style abound in novels of the period, especially in the work of Sir Walter Scott.

As adapted to the row house, the Gothic Revival style employed Tudor arches with carved spandrels to replace pilastered doorways, slender clustered colonnettes flanking the sliding doors between parlors, medieval window tracery, and medieval ceiling centerpieces and railings.

Unlike the Greek Revival style, Gothic Revival lasted through the years of the Civil War, finally evolving into what has been called the Ruskinian or Venetian Gothic.

The Gothic Revival style. The mansion on the left, in a photograph taken in 1891, still stands in Gramercy Park. The alternating light and dark stones in the window arches are Venetian in feeling; such late examples of the style are sometimes called Venetian Gothic. The house on the right, originally a rectory, is unmistakably Gothic, with its pointed arches and heavy moldings.

The Romanesque Revival style. The most prominent feature is the round arch, and naturalistic sculptural forms are typical. The row shown here is in Brooklyn's Park Slope, which has hundreds of well-maintained houses built when the style was fashionable.

ROMANESQUE REVIVAL (1844-1900)

The Romanesque Revival style, so heavy and ponderous that it was employed mostly in large public buildings, is not often seen in row houses. Its foremost advocate in America was the Boston architect Henry Hobson Richardson, designer of the famous Trinity Church. Because of his influence, the style is often called Richardsonian Romanesque. Heavy masonry walls interrupted by occasional round-headed openings, these framed with moldings or wide bands of low-relief carvings, distinguish this style. Colonnettes frame the doorways, and there was considerable freedom in design of massive ironwork.

The first building constructed in this style in America is the Church of the Pilgrims (now Our Lady of Lebanon) at Henry and Remsen Streets in New York's Brooklyn Heights. Brooklyn Heights has several other examples of Romanesque Revival, among them the celebrated Herman Behr house at the corner of Pierpont and Henry Streets, built of stone, brick, terracotta, and tile in 1890 by the architect Frank Freeman.

An unusual detail on a Romanesque Revival doorway. The head on the left seems to be an idealized figure, but the one on the right suggests a portrait of the owner—or perhaps the architect.

35

More Romanesque Revival. In the rendering, the applied pilasters and the banding are Romanesque, although the style has been modified. In the photograph on this page, round and segmental arches and rough ashlar base courses suggest medieval forms. Single panes of glass, replacing sashed windows, emphasize the elements of the design. The details on the next page are typical: delicately carved bas-relief, intricate ironwork, short fluted columns flanking the windows. The single griffin at upper left reflects the asymmetrical design notions of the Romanesque.

ITALIANATE (1849-1860)

The mid-nineteenth-century Italianate style was as simple and plain as the Greek, Gothic, and Romanesque styles were ornate. It took as its model the austere Italian house that sheltered most of Italy's population, a house that maintained certain basic features dating to the Etruscan and early Roman periods. These features included plain, stuccoed walls, clean-cut windows, and low-pitched roofs with deep overhanging eaves supported on brackets.

The Italianate style. The contemporary rendering for a double house in Boston shows a very free use of medieval forms. The photograph of the facade of a wooden house in San Francisco—now demolished—shows a mixture of medieval and classical detail. The workability of wood allowed great exuberance of expression.

More Italianate. The style was popular just after the Civil War, coincidental with an urban housing boom, and consequently many examples remain. Note that the drawing shows two "half houses" —each 12½ feet wide and sharing a 25-foot plot. The photograph on this page shows three row houses that express the style in its simplest and purest form. The Park Slope houses in the photograph on the next page use the style more freely, and there is machine-cut decoration which was the landmark of the Eastlake style, but there is the same emphasis on vertical line.

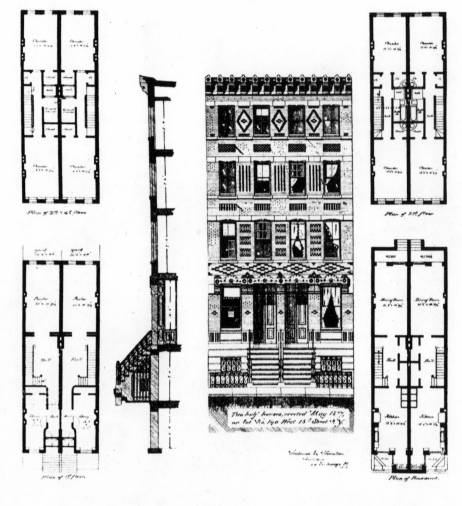

The style was first seen in the United States in a line drawing by architect John Haviland in his book *The Builder's Assistant,* which appeared from 1818 to 1821. The drawing portrays a two-storied residence with a recessed entrance in a gabled pavilion, with small, one-storied wings on each side, adorned only by small columns at the entrance, and beam ends supporting thin cornices.

Row houses in this style are immediately noticeable for their simplicity of architectural detail. Even ironwork fences and stair railings have been kept to the strictest designs.

The Renaissance Revival style. The two photographs directly below, taken in 1891, show new houses. The Romanesque influence is apparent, but every detail is a Renaissance motif—garlands, shields, acanthus bands. The house in the photograph at the bottom is yellow brick with precast limestone details. On the next page, a row of Renaissance Revival houses with low stoops and center entrances. Heavy entablatures, quoins, and cornices make this row on Manhattan's Upper West Side unique.

RENAISSANCE REVIVAL (1850-1900)

Like the Italianate style, the Renaissance Revival style was modeled after the houses of Italy. While the Italianate style was copied from the homes of the Italian lower and middle class, however, the Renaissance Revival style captured the architecture of the nobility. As a result, it was marked by opulence, a concern for detail, and lavish scale.

In the row house, the grand scale was simulated by extreme ceiling heights. Ornamentation was abundant; capitals, friezes, and consoles were embellished with lush carvings. To add diversity to the somewhat regular pattern of the row house, different cornices were often employed over the windows of every story.

Brownstone was one of the most popular building materials used in row houses of the Renaissance Revival style. Since it was porous and difficult to carve, however, architectural details were often made of cast iron. Successive coats of paint and sand were then added to the cast iron, and the finished product was hardly distinguishable from the stone. This technique was usually employed on stair rails and balusters.

More Renaissance Revival—a profusion of Renaissance figures. The row on this page, now demolished, demonstrates the adaptability of the style to wood construction.

The Queen Anne style. Features include isolated bay windows, an asymmetrical use of all elements, and paneled insets of bas-relief.

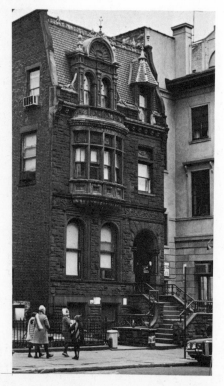

QUEEN ANNE (1880-1900)

Unlike the Revival styles, which to some extent followed certain patterns, the Queen Anne style was a catch-all form of architecture, a mixture of styles that adopted elements from widely diverse periods. It depended on unusual mixtures of forms, colors, and textures. It took its name from the queen who ruled England at the beginning of the eighteenth century, yet it employed many of the features found in buildings constructed during the Stuart reign in the seventeenth century.

Typical Queen Anne features are medieval-type pargeting and gabled roofing, flat bay windows, and mixtures of rectangular, arched, and elliptical openings. One distinguishing mark of the period is a decorative device associated with the English architect Sir Charles Eastlake. It consisted of a long, flat molding, usually displaying a reeded central section, that was used both in furniture and the interior of buildings. Carved foliage designs also appeared on stone lintels and over-door friezes both interior and exterior. Windows were large; bay windows were common, with two or three planes to the bay. Turrets and dormers were used on corners and roofs.

The Colonial Revival style. Two of the houses pictured here are superb examples.

A pair of buildings, one of them tastelessly translated into Colonial Revival. The house on the left, recently remodeled in the French Provincial style, is far more successful.

COLONIAL REVIVAL (1890-1940)

The Colonial Revival style, like most, was imitative, but it had one distinguishing factor—it imitated indigenous American designs. Its beginning can be traced to the noted tour made by the architectural firm of McKim, Mead, Bigelow, and White in 1877. On this tour the Georgian houses of New England were examined and studied.

Most evident in this style was the inclusion of features taken from the colonial period on houses of improper scale. Details were often badly out of scale with the facade of the house—columns in doorways grossly oversized, undersized transoms, relief moldings under modillions that were so small that they are barely distinguishable.

Often features were borrowed from other houses on the same street, and almost invariably they looked better on the earlier houses. This style still persists; it remains the dream of many a potential house owner. But good Colonial Revival architecture has become prohibitively expensive to build—which will speed the development of a simpler style that is presently evolving.

MODERN

The Modern style. This house, built by an architect for his own use, is an interesting solution to the exterior design problem, although the International style details now are somewhat dated.

Modern or contemporary row houses are distinguished by clean lines, simplicity of design, and a free approach to the use of color and space. Much as the Gothic row house was influenced by the towering spires of medieval churches, modern row houses have grown out of the spare steel-and-glass designs of skyscrapers.

Most noticeable in modern row houses has been the substitution of new materials for the traditional brownstone, limestone, brick, and wood. Concrete, glass block, stucco, steel, mosaic tile, and aluminum are used. Brick is sometimes employed, but as a decorative rather than a structural material.

Perhaps the most striking feature of modern row-house design is the use of interpenetrating spaces. Ceilings are frequently two and three stories high, and light wells penetrate from ground floor to roof. Skylights are common, and also central staircases, which free interior walls.

Narrow brick ends flank corrugated asbestos spandrels and horizontal casement windows—a straightforward design particularly suitable for the narrow row house.

Less suitable would seem to be amber-colored Plexiglas insets in place of conventional window openings. It is a daring attempt at originality—but what one first notices about the house is the stain marks on the flat stucco facade under each bubble.

TWO|NEIGHBORHOODS

Some city neighborhoods, like New York's Brooklyn Heights, Chicago's Near North, and Washington's Georgetown, are world-famous. Others are virtually unheard-of, even by residents of the city of which they are a part. In some well-established neighborhoods a row house will cost several hundred thousand dollars. In others, houses can still be purchased for as little as five thousand dollars. Cost aside, each city neighborhood has a distinct personality, and an understanding of the personality of the neighborhood you will live in is a vital part of becoming a city homeowner. Like it or not, the neighborhood is an extension of the house you may buy, as important as that spacious living room or carved mantelpiece.

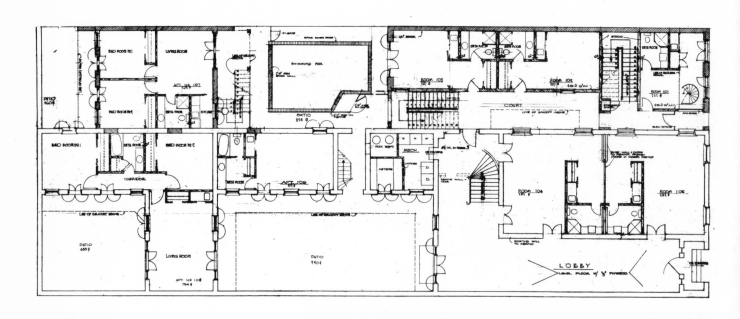

New Orleans row houses remodeled to contain six apartments. In the Vieux Carré all facades must conform to the New Orleans style. The larger house on the left is original; the one on the right is a recent addition.

A city neighborhood can be a brilliant mix of styles and urban forms. As the pattern of each neighborhood evolves, apartment houses take over the ends of the block and row houses remain in the middle, thereby preserving low open areas in the quieter part of the neighborhood while permitting high-density housing on the busy avenues.

A row-house neighborhood in Albany, showing various remodeling conceptions. Three of the houses are basically the same, but each owner has expressed his individual taste.

Most neighborhoods where row houses are available at reasonable prices will be run-down and impoverished, slums or near-slums. It is a discouraging reality of present-day row-house living. Neighborhoods can and do change, however, and the influx of new people, buying and renovating row houses, is the most evident sign of a neighborhood's rejuvenation. The most fashionable urban neighborhoods—neighborhoods like Brooklyn Heights, where houses, when they are available, sell for upwards of $100,000—were on their way to becoming slums until a few enterprising individuals recognized the intrinsic value of their row houses.

Evaluating a neighborhood therefore includes not only an analysis of the neighborhood as it now exists but an estimate of what the neighborhood may become. There are many factors involved in such an evaluation, among them the appearance of the neighborhood, the presence of landmarks and monuments, the availability of public assistance under urban-renewal and other programs, zoning, schools, goods and services, transportation, and finally the people who live in the neighborhood, your neighbors.

Choosing a neighborhood is a highly personal decision. A neighborhood perfect for one family may be quite wrong for another. You must decide what your needs are and how you want to live, and then select a neighborhood that will suit you, if not now at least in the near future.

THE LOOK OF A NEIGHBORHOOD

When you go out to inspect a house you should take a casual walk through the neighborhood, to get the feel of it. Does it have an identity? Is there some special quality that appeals to you? What was it like fifty years ago? What was it like *five* years ago? Is it on the way up or is it deteriorating? Neighborhoods can change drastically. Elegant neighborhoods have become slums, and many run-down neighborhoods, thanks to the efforts of dedicated residents, have become

A beautifully remodeled brownstone—a credit to any neighborhood.

charming, beautiful communities. Remember that if you move into the neighborhood you yourself will represent a change. Carefully examine its condition and estimate what you can do to improve it.

You will want to look for row houses already renovated or under renovation. They will give you a clear picture of what the house you are considering could become. And don't necessarily be discouraged if there has been little renovation in the neighborhood: someone has to be a pioneer, and in neighborhoods where there has been little renovation prices are usually low.

Features such as parks and playgrounds are important, especially if you have children or dogs that demand exercise. Any feature that breaks the monotony and boredom imposed by the grid pattern of most cities—curving streets, unusually shaped buildings, fountains, or hills—should be considered a plus.

LANDMARKS AND HISTORIC DISTRICTS

One real bonus to a neighborhood is the presence of an acknowledged landmark, a structure with some special architectural or historical significance. Landmarks enhance the appearance of a neighborhood and give it a sense of history. They can be a real economic benefit, supporting property values and assuring a solid tax base. They also generate tourism, bringing money into the neighborhood.

Until recent years, however, landmarks were largely unprotected, and many historic buildings were razed in the name of progress. New York City is a prime example of this unfortunate destruction. In Manhattan, for example, there are no seventeenth-century structures still standing and only a few from the eighteenth century. Luckily, this landmark razing has since been quelled, thanks to national, state, and municipal programs and legislation and to the efforts of private preservation groups.

One of the most significant results of landmark preservation at the city level has been the recognition of historic districts. Historic districts are not individual landmarks but specific areas of a city, ranging in size from three or four blocks to fifty blocks or more. Notable examples of historic districts are Brooklyn Heights and Greenwich Village in New York, Beacon Hill in Boston, Georgetown in Washington, and Russian Hill in San Francisco.

In historic districts that have been legally designated, a special zoning ordinance imposes architectural controls over the alteration, demolition, and construction of buildings. The typical ordinance requires owners to submit architectural plans to an administrative board, which must issue a permit before the external appearance of the building is changed.

Many of these administrative boards—such as the New York City Landmarks Preservation Commission—offer consulting work free of charge to owners in historic districts. In New York's Greenwich Village, for example, the owner of a haberdashery recently moved his store to a building constructed in 1853 for an uncle of the novelist Henry James. Aided by the city's Landmarks Preservation Commission, the shopowner designed a modern storefront that retained the Anglo-Italianate feeling of the building. Recently the Association of Village Homeowners awarded its first citation to the shopowner for distinguished commercial alteration.

The former Russian Embassy in New York, now an important landmark, was about to be demolished when it was saved by private funds and eventually restored. The interior was meticulously restored to its original design. It is hardly a row house, but every row house for blocks around benefits by its presence.

The West Side Urban Renewal Area in Manhattan. A few years ago the row houses could be had for a few thousand dollars. Now one of these houses, remodeled, sells for more than a hundred thousand dollars, and the neighborhood is alive again.

URBAN-RENEWAL AREAS

Most major cities have neighborhoods that have been designated urban-renewal areas. The housing in these areas, because of overcrowding and misuse, has deteriorated. To rehabilitate these houses, the cities, assisted by federal and state governments, have set standards for property improvement and offered financial assistance as well as tax abatements and exemptions. Where the owner cannot or will not make the required improvements, the cities are empowered to acquire the properties and sell them to new owners who will make the improvements.

There are disadvantages to buying and renovating a house in an urban-renewal area, but they are slight compared with the advantages. If you acquire such a house you can expect frustrating delays in appraisals and approval of plans, and infuriating encounters with well-meaning but inexperienced officials. But in most urban-renewal areas it is possible to get mortgages at exceptionally low interest rates, and this alone makes the red tape worth the trouble. Another important advantage is that you know the neighborhood is going to be improved, whereas in a non-renewal neighborhood you can only hope that individuals like yourself will cause a gradual improvement.

ZONING

Some neighborhoods, although zoned commercially, have been maintained as residential areas. You should make yourself well aware of the zoning restrictions before purchasing a house. A commercially zoned neighborhood would allow you to open a restaurant in your row house or set up a "cottage industry"—a cabinet-making shop, a handmade-textile shop, a gourmet shop. It might also allow a department store or supermarket to become your next-door neighbor.

Residentially zoned neighborhoods may vary; in some there may be restrictions on the height of buildings, to prevent developers from turning blocks of row houses and carriage houses into looming apartment houses. The same restrictions might prevent you from building a greenhouse on your roof. If the zoning restrictions of a particular neighborhood would prevent you from using your property the way you want to or would not protect you from unwelcome changes, you would be wise to think twice about the house, difficult as it may be to cross off a neighborhood that looks suitable at the moment.

SCHOOLS

If you have children or plan to have them, schools are obviously an important factor in evaluating a neighborhood. It is an unfortunate reality that schools in many deteriorated neighborhoods are decidedly inferior, despite attempts to equalize educational opportunities. And waiting for schools to improve is no solution for families with school-age children. Private schools are an alternative, but unless your children already go to private schools, you should add the very large cost of private education to the other costs—buying, renovating, monthly payments, maintenance—before you decide you can afford a city house. If you want to send your children to public schools, you should certainly talk to parents in the neighborhood and do any other research you can. You may find that the school is quite acceptable; you may find that though it is not a good school it is improving rapidly, perhaps as a by-product of neighborhood rehabilitation; you may find that at least at the present time you are not willing to send your children there.

GOODS AND SERVICES

Perhaps the most common complaint among row-house owners is the lack of goods and services in their neighborhoods. The reason is that the renovation of city neighborhoods is a fairly recent development. The absence of good basic stores can be a serious problem. But the lack of such specialized goods and services as bookstores, gourmet shops, restaurants, and theaters is no reason to rule a neighborhood out. As the demand increases, these specialized goods and services will appear. In fact, some brownstone owners have attacked the problem directly, by opening "cottage industries" on the ground floor of their houses.

New York's Upper West Side is an excellent example of how the kind and quality of goods and services can change as the population of a neighborhood changes. Once one of the city's most elegant neighborhoods, the Upper West Side suffered years of slow deterioration. Much of the area turned to single-room occupancy, and there were few stores, theaters, or good restaurants. A few years ago, however, the availability of large, inexpensive apartments and the designation of a large portion of the area as an urban renewal district began to attract large numbers of New Yorkers who had never before considered the Upper West Side, among them writers, artists, professional people, and a host of young families. Specialty goods and services soon began to appear. Now the Upper West Side abounds in fine restaurants, boutiques, gourmet shops, and small theaters. Prices, inevitably, have increased.

Basic goods and services, however, should be evaluated before you decide on a neighborhood. Food shopping is one important factor. Small grocery stores are fine, but if you have a family to feed you will be hoping for at least one supermarket. And prices of foodstuffs are to be considered. The cost of a tomato may easily double from one neighborhood to another.

The reliability of garbage collection is another important issue. Moving from an apartment building where garbage is collected every day to a row-house neighborhood where the garbage truck visits only twice a week can be upsetting.

And if you are planning on extensive remodeling or renovation—and doing the work yourself—a nearby hardware or building-supply store is a must.

TRANSPORTATION

One of the obvious advantages of the city house is its accessibility—to your job, to shopping, to theaters and museums, to all the benefits the city has to offer. As a city homeowner you will inevitably experience a surge of relief when you see your suburban friends rush to catch the 6:05, prepared to spend an hour or more standing on a crowded train, gulping Scotch out of paper cups if they are lucky. But if you yourself have to catch two buses and then walk ten blocks—perhaps in rain or snow—to get to your row house, much of this advantage will have been lost.

When you are seriously considering a house, always make a visit to it by public transportation. Discover the accessibility of the house right from the beginning. Check schedules to see how often, and at what hours, trains and buses run. In some areas of many cities service stops after midnight, meaning that you will have to pay a hefty taxi fare every time you decide to stay out late. Also be sure to check alternate modes of transportation. It can be very convenient to have both subway and bus service.

The quality of a neighborhood's public transporation is so important that it often affects the price of a house. Prices are noticeably higher in areas where transportation is good. Many prospective buyers have avoided New York's Lower East Side precisely because public transportation in the neighborhood is poor.

If you own an automobile, parking can be another consideration. Will alternate-side-of-the-street parking regulations mean that you must spend an hour each day trying to find a place for your car? Garages are an obvious solution to parking problems and are a cost that should be included in your budget analysis. There may be local commercial garages, but check their rates.

NEIGHBORS

A few years ago, before buying a row house in a charming neighborhood in Brooklyn, a New Yorker said: "I'd really love to buy a brownstone but the ones I like and can afford are in Brooklyn, and my friends will never come to visit." Despite this common complaint, he went ahead and bought the house and settled down to a year of painting, sanding, hammering, scraping, and scrubbing. During this time he had little chance to even consider seeing his Manhattan friends. Virtually the only people he saw were his neighbors—to ask for advice on how to plaster this, to borrow a tool to refinish that. By the end of the year he found that his neighbors *were* his friends. He also discovered that many of his Manhattan friends, after seeing the fruits of his labors, were looking for houses in his neighborhood.

The people who live in a neighborhood, your prospective neighbors, will be a vital part of your venture into city house living. Obviously you cannot inspect and evaluate them as you would a building or a supermarket. Nevertheless, you should try to talk to as many people in the neighborhood as you can before deciding on a house. Most row-house neighborhoods have some sort of organization or association, and if the neighborhood you are considering has one you should definitely attend one of their meetings. They will welcome you, and it is by far the best way to meet your future neighbors.

You can expect to find some variety in almost any row-house neighborhood—social, economic, and ethnic. Most city dwellers not only are willing to accept this variety but look forward to it; it is part of city living and is certainly part of neighborhood rehabilitation. If a neighborhood is abjectly poor, with no economic mix at all, your purchase of a house will make you a real pioneer, and you must expect some hardships. You may be the only homeowner for blocks around—the only person in the neighborhood with more than a rent-payer's interest in it. The house may be charming. Your purchase may attract other pioneers and lead eventually to a better neighborhood, but it will take several years.

NEIGHBORHOOD ASSOCIATIONS

Neighborhood associations are composed of concerned residents who have banded together to combat deterioration in their neighborhood and to provide themselves with a forum in which they can discuss common problems and the means of solving them. Some neighborhood associations are enormously effective, others are merely token groups. Perhaps the highest recommendation a neighborhood can have is a strong and active association.

Neighborhood associations have been effective in several areas. Several groups in Brooklyn's Park Slope and Boerum Hill have held "Saturday Sweeps" where local residents, aided by the city's sanitation men, clean the neighborhood's areaways, sidewalks, and gutters. The police department restricts parking for the day, and the district sanitation superintendent contributes a sweeper, flusher, brooms, a truck, and posters. The Director of Sanitary Education will supply an association with a film displaying cleaning techniques, and the Sani-

These simple porched houses in Clinton Hill have been maintained in their original form and in excellent condition ever since they were built—a sign that the community is stable.

Beacon Hill has a charm and scale unequaled in this country. Red brick facades front on a red brick sidewalk sloping down to other streets.

tation Department has even sent its sound truck, "The Voice of Cleanliness," to lend verbal and musical encouragement. Such clean-ups, incidentally, can happen even without such organization, in a block that is in transition. If one or two homeowners begin sweeping the gutters on a Saturday morning, within a few minutes others will join in—especially if it's a nice sunny day.

One very popular association activity is the block party. Police close the block, and the association sponsors pet shows, art sales, athletic contests, and so on. Refreshments are sold, and often local merchants donate merchandise for an auction. Proceeds from the block party are used to plant trees on the street, to provide plots of flowers for a neighboring park, or for other projects. Such a block party may seem trivial, but it is not. It is a sign of health in a neighborhood, and it becomes a happy part of the neighborhood's history.

Other association activities include historical research, house tours, establishing youth groups and educational centers, and publishing neighborhood newspapers.

SOME NOTABLE NEIGHBORHOODS

The remainder of this chapter is a collection of sketches of some row-house neighborhoods—some well known, some not so well known. All of them are of interest to the prospective buyer, whether he is looking for an ideal house in a fine neighborhood or a forlorn rooming house begging to be restored to livability. But there are many, many more neighborhoods, in New York, Boston, Baltimore, Philadelphia, New Haven, St. Louis, Rochester, Albany, and other cities. I am most familiar with Brooklyn, where several neighborhoods have recently emerged, each with a distinct character and with well-designed nineteenth-century houses—Fort Greene, Clinton Hill, Crown Heights, the Prospect-Lefferts Gardens area near the Botanic Gardens, and so on. Many houses are available in these neighborhoods for about $25,000, and there are other Brooklyn neighborhoods, on the verge of discovery, where houses are considerably cheaper.

This elegantly maintained Georgian house faces Boston Common. It is part of several blocks of the earliest and most striking row houses in America.

BEACON HILL

Boston's Beacon Hill, named for a warning beacon placed on the summit in 1634, was originally used as pastureland for horses and cattle. Development began in 1795 when the architect Charles Bulfinch erected the historic State House. Beacon Hill quickly became the most fashionable, sought-after section of Boston.

Around 1860, however, the newly filled Back Bay began to challenge Beacon Hill's supremacy. Houses began to deteriorate and property values sharply declined. Then, around the turn of the century, Beacon Hill was rediscovered and its houses restored, making it one of the first neighborhoods in the nation to undergo restoration. Property values have been climbing ever since. One house on Louisburg Square sold for $15,000 in 1910. In 1920 the price was $24,000; in 1931, $34,000; and today the house is valued at $140,000.

Beacon Hill was made a historic district in 1955, and in 1963 the Department of the Interior designated it a National Historic Landmark. Today, along Beacon Hill's narrow, tree-lined streets stand some of the country's most beautifully restored row houses.

SOUTH END

Within walking distance of downtown Boston, the South End was once an elegant neighborhood, laced with row after row of bow-fronted, red-brick, four-story nineteenth-century houses. By 1885, however, the affluent had abandoned the neighborhood, moving across Commonwealth Avenue to the banks of the Charles River. The neighborhood quickly deteriorated and the graceful, spacious townhouses were converted to rooming houses run by absentee landlords.

Then, in the early 1960s, a few enterprising families realized that the South End offered comfortable city living at low cost, often for no more than back taxes. The houses boasted fine marble fireplaces, lofty, elegantly embellished ceilings, and handsome woodwork hidden by only a few coats of paint.

The move to the South End has continued—an estimated 25 percent of Boston's architects live there, for example—but the neighborhood has by no means been completely renovated. It still has the largest rooming house population in Boston, and poverty is still very evident. And the less affluent residents of the South End have banded together to prevent the takeover of the neighborhood by the new homeowners. The poor, who moved into the neighborhood when it was originally abandoned by the rich, are determined to stay there. It is a problem faced by many neighborhoods undergoing rehabilitation and one not likely to be solved without the construction of new housing in vast quantity. The South End is beset with other problems: new highways and by-passes and stretches of depressed railroads encircle the neighborhood, cutting it off from the rest of the city. New air rights over these obstacles promise to relieve this condition, but the neighborhood still has a steep climb ahead of it.

Handsome, spacious, four-story houses can still be purchased in the South End for under $20,000, however, and as long as such bargains are available people will continue to move in. The South End is a striking example of a neighborhood in transition.

In Boston's South End, houses are often set back to provide open green areas. Many of the houses have a smooth granite base course and brick above. They were built in larger groups than houses in New York and other cities, resulting in a more controlled streetscape. The details show a particular freedom in the use of classical forms.

WOOSTER SQUARE

Wooster Square, before and after. The only unattractive element is the overhead electric wires.

Wooster Square, one of New Haven's residential neighborhoods, is an excellent example of how federal assistance can help uplift a deteriorating neighborhood. Once a fashionable suburb, the neighborhood is still graced with old mansions facing a handsome green. Reflecting somewhat grimmer days, it is also pocked with shabby loft factories and crumbling tenements.

In 1959 Wooster Square became a federally aided urban-renewal project. The loft factories are now being razed and some 440 buildings are marked for rehabilitation. And the urban-renewal project has offered homeowners numerous other advantages. Mortgages are now available at low interest rates where it was impossible to obtain mortgages before. New stores, parks, a community-center school, a fire station, landscaped parking lots, and a new streetlighting system are being constructed and trees are being planted. Improved police and fire protection as well as improved street cleaning and garbage collection are being provided. And the city of New Haven itself has purchased and rehabilitated fourteen neglected buildings to dramatically demonstrate the possibilities of renovation in Wooster Square. It is now a neighborhood on the way up.

Before and after in Philadelphia's Old City. These are not just renovations but painstaking restorations.

PHILADELPHIA—OLD CITY

Old City was "downtown" Philadelphia in Ben Franklin's time but the present-day downtown is a bit to the east. There are as many as 650 houses in this area to be restored, and about a hundred have been completed. Perhaps another 250 are being restored by their owners; most of them are "certified" historic houses and renovation must be approved by a commission. Much of this program is supported by federal renewal funds. The houses are sold to individuals for about $30,000—not much more expensive, considering lower city taxes and no commuting, than owning a house in the suburbs. Land values are rising—and Old City looks like a real success story, though similar things are happening in many other historic urban areas throughout the country.

Chelsea is still a mix of rooming houses and privately owned homes. These Federal houses have only recently been reclaimed by homeowners.

CHELSEA

Chelsea is a neighborhood on Manhattan's West Side, stretching roughly from 14th Street to 30th Street. Into the 1950's Chelsea's hundreds of rooming houses served as clearing houses for new arrivals in the city. Now, thanks to the trend toward row-house rehabilitation, entire blocks of Chelsea are covered with handsomely renovated homes, most of them constructed around the middle of the nineteenth century.

One of the major features of Chelsea is its excellent transportation. All three of New York's subway systems service the neighborhood, and there is good bus service on the avenues that slice through it. It is within walking distance of midtown Manhattan.

Chelsea boasts some stabilizing landmarks, among them the General Theological Seminary on Ninth Avenue and the historic Chelsea Hotel, on 23rd Street, a favorite of New York writers and composers.

There is strong community sentiment among Chelsea residents. The neighborhood has several experimental theater and dance groups and sponsors an annual art show. It also has a neighborhood newspaper, the *Chelsea Clinton News*, which provides a good source of information about the area.

The neighborhood faces several serious problems. There is a need for playground and park space (local groups are trying desperately to obtain space along the Hudson River shore to the west for recreational use), and financing is difficult in the neighborhood. Mortgages rarely cover more than the value assessed by the city for tax purposes, usually about 50 per cent of the actual market value of the property. At this writing, houses in Chelsea can be found for as little as $25,000, though some top the $100,000 mark.

A pleasant corner in Brooklyn Heights. The rear windows of this row of houses overlook New York Harbor and lower Manhattan.

BROOKLYN HEIGHTS

Just over the Brooklyn Bridge from New York's City Hall, across the East River from the Wall Street financial district, Brooklyn Heights is the model for row-house renovation in New York. Like most row-house neighborhoods, Brooklyn Heights was on the way down when, in the 1950s, the value of its fine homes was recognized. Now it is almost completely renovated. Beautiful brownstone, limestone, and brick row houses, punctuated with an occasional alley or carriage house, flank its tree-lined streets and stone-paved sidewalks. Most notable in Brooklyn Heights is the graceful Esplanade, which circles its northwestern edge, providing a dramatic view of Manhattan and New York Harbor.

Today Brooklyn Heights is a Historic Landmark Area and has also been designated a National Historic Site by the Department of the Interior. Houses once could be purchased for as little as $20,000, but no such bargains exist today. For most prospective city homeowners, Brooklyn Heights can be only an example of what a neighborhood can someday become.

Typical of successful row-house neighborhoods, Brooklyn Heights has an energetic, effective community organization, the Brooklyn Heights Association, founded in 1910. The association has some 1,500 members and sponsors a historic preservation committee and a design advisory council to aid owners in property improvement, as well as committees on education, police, housing, urban renewal, cleanliness, and other community concerns.

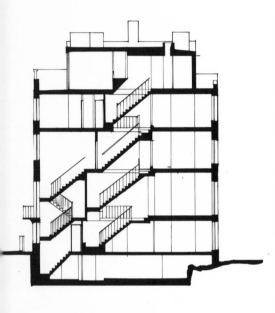

A remodeled house in Turtle Bay with an ingenious stair arrangement. From the outside it is an imposing mansion; inside are two completely private multifloor units.

TURTLE BAY

It is hard to believe that Turtle Bay, that small portion of New York that runs from 49th Street to 51st Street and from the East River to Third Avenue, was ever anything but a luxurious, expensive neighborhood. Yet in the early years of this century Turtle Bay was deteriorating, a neighborhood consisting of run-down brownstones, flour mills, tanneries, breweries, and slaughterhouses. Elevated railroads over Third and Second Avenues spewed soot and ash as they noisily clattered along. Cheap restaurants, gin mills, second-hand stores, and pawn shops abounded.

Around the end of the First World War, however, the neighborhood began to change. About 1920, for example, Mrs. Walton Marton purchased twenty houses—ten facing north on 49th Street and ten south on 48th Street—and, under the guidance of the architect Clarence Dean, restored them to form Turtle Bay Gardens. Among the noted residents were E. B. White of *The New Yorker,* Scribner's celebrated editor Maxwell Perkins, the conductor Leopold Stokowski, Ambassador Phillip C. Jessup, Tyrone Power, and Katharine Hepburn. In 1926 the violinist Efrem Zimbalist built a house at 225-227 East 49th Street. He lived there with his wife, the celebrated opera star Alma Gluck, and his daughter, the novelist Marcia Davenport. Later the house was occupied by Henry Luce, the founder of *Time-Life.* Strangely enough, this lavish house was gutted in 1957 to form the 17th Police Precinct Station House.

Today Turtle Bay is still the home of the rich and famous. Many of its brownstones contain elegant restaurants, and the second-hand stores of old are now expensive antique shops. Its row houses are beyond compare.

BOERUM HILL

Boerum Hill had been a bypassed neighborhood for many decades when it began to come alive. This had some advantages: no money had ever been spent on faddish remodeling. The three-story houses shown here originally had wooden porches like those shown earlier in this chapter in Clinton Hill. The porches were not maintained, and it would be impractical to restore them now. The present owners have made the best of the very considerable virtues that the houses retain; the particular block above is one of the restoration spearheads in the area and has been widely publicized.

Boerum Hill borders the southern edge of downtown Brooklyn and is a neighborhood that has recently undergone extensive renovation. Greek Revival, Federal, and Victorian brownstones can still be found in this neighborhood for low prices, and new families are moving in almost daily.

One of Boerum Hill's attractions is its proximity to downtown Brooklyn and its excellent transportation into midtown Manhattan. Boerum Hill is serviced by eight subway systems as well as the Long Island Railroad. No point in the neighborhood is more than four blocks from at least one Manhattan-bound subway.

Two areas of Boerum Hill have been designated as landmark districts and another portion is expected to be designated in the near future.

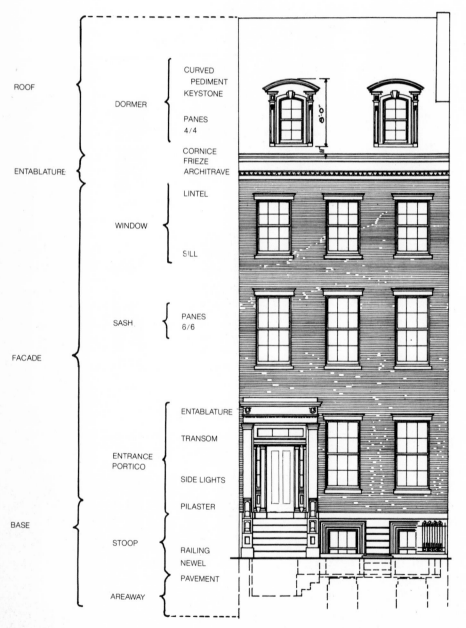

ROOF

ENTABLATURE

FACADE

BASE

DORMER { CURVED
PEDIMENT
KEYSTONE

PANES
4/4

CORNICE
FRIEZE
ARCHITRAVE

WINDOW { LINTEL

SILL

SASH { PANES
6/6

ENTRANCE
PORTICO { ENTABLATURE

TRANSOM

SIDE LIGHTS

PILASTER

STOOP { RAILING
NEWEL
PAVEMENT

AREAWAY

6'0"

Greenwich Village has both small row houses built
early in the nineteenth century and larger ones
built somewhat later. These two drawings are to
the same scale.

H.A.B.S.

A row of very early houses on Charlton Street in Greenwich Village. The house in the foreground has received a citation from the Association of Village Homeowners for its remodeling.

GREENWICH VILLAGE

Bounded by 14th Street, Fifth Avenue, Houston Street, and Hudson Street, Greenwich Village contains many of New York City's finest eighteenth- and nineteenth-century homes. Early in the century the Village was a flourishing artists' colony and acquired an aura of glamour and romance. The artists have long since fled, seeking less expensive neighborhoods, but the Village has desperately held on to its past reputation.

The principal landmark in the Village is Washington Square with its classic arch, and until the 1950s the Square was surrounded with row houses. In this decade, however, an entire block was demolished and replaced by luxury high-rise apartments. There followed a wave of luxury apartment construction—the buildings were given names like Van Gogh and Matisse to capitalize on the Village's artistic reputation—which was not quelled until the area was finally proclaimed a landmark district.

The Village contains many of the city's finest restaurants and shops, and is one of the last strongholds of real individuality in Manhattan. There are still row houses available along its narrow, curving streets, but they are quite expensive and usually require considerable remodeling to restore.

Park Slope is almost a museum of isolated nineteenth-century styles. In this Italianate row, there is untouched brownstone, restored brownstone, and painted brownstone.

PARK SLOPE

One urban planner called Park Slope "the most beautiful Victorian area on the East Coast, probably in the United States." A long, narrow area that runs for some twenty blocks along the western edge of Brooklyn's Prospect Park—it is only five blocks wide, allowing all neighborhood residents access to the park—the neighborhood has always been a stable middle-class community, and is now being invaded by a host of architects, lawyers, businessmen, artists, and writers.

Park Slope row houses, still available at reasonable prices, boast incredible interiors—living rooms 30 to 40 feet long with 13-foot-high ceilings, wood paneling, Victorian dressing rooms complete with marble sinks, pier glasses, stained-glass windows, mahogany sliding doors, and often original gas fixtures and chandeliers.

THREE | THE RIGHT HOUSE FOR YOU

Perhaps the most exciting stage of becoming a city homeowner is the looking. There are dozens of possibilities, and no commitment. It is fine to enjoy looking, but if you are seriously interested in buying a house, you should try to be systematic.

Looking for a city house is a twofold process. First you must find a house that suits your tastes and needs, or can be made to suit them. Then you must carefully evaluate the condition of the house to determine whether you can, in fact, afford both the purchase and the renovation.

A beautiful Gothic-style house in dire condition. Money and energy would reap remarkable rewards here, and it is surprising that no one yet has invested them. The house has many interesting details, such as the quatrefoil railing, ogee bargeboard, and quatrefoil attic lights.

Obviously a knowledge of architecture, real-estate law, and engineering would be helpful in finding and evaluating a house, but few prospective city home-owners are so equipped. There are, however, several steps you can take that will make your search easier and more profitable.

Carefully determine your financial capabilities. Know exactly what you can afford to spend, both to purchase the house and then to make it habitable.

Know what kind of structure you are looking for. Size and type of architecture are only part of this determination. Do you want a house that requires only minor, "cosmetic" repairs to make it habitable, or a house that demands extensive renovation? Both offer numerous advantages and disadvantages.

Enlist expert advice whenever possible. The opinions of architects, engineers, and people who have already bought and renovated city houses can be invaluable.

Finally, look at as many houses as you possibly can, even before making up your mind what you really want. You will learn from each house you inspect.

WHAT YOU CAN AFFORD

The accepted rule of thumb is that you can probably afford to spend about two and a half times your net yearly income on a city house. This is based on a total figure, including renovation costs as well as the sale price of the house. But as you will most likely buy your house on time, it is perhaps more meaningful to compute monthly payments—a composite of mortgage, taxes, heating, maintenance, insurance, and loan-payment costs—when deciding what you can afford. Monthly payments amounting to one quarter of your net monthly income are usually considered acceptable.

It must be said, however, that these figures are merely guidelines. Life styles vary widely, and while some prospective homeowners can afford a considerably larger percentage of income, others would find themselves financially strapped even at a smaller percentage. (In the next chapter I deal with the financial aspects of buying a city house in more detail.)

"MOVE-IN," "NEEDS REMODELING," OR "SHELL"

There are three basic types of city houses available to the prospective home-owner. These can be described, as they are in most real estate ads, as "move-in," "needs remodeling," or "shell." (Chapter Five discusses each type of house.) Even before beginning your search, you can examine the possibilities of these vastly different types of houses and select the type that is best suited to you. The others you can eliminate immediately, greatly simplifying your search. However, many people begin with quite vague ideas about what they want and can decide on a "move-in" or "shell" house only after they have considered specific possibilities and problems with houses they have seen.

EXPERTS

Few people who buy automobiles know much about transmissions and valves, and few people who purchase city houses know much about supporting walls and electrical systems. When you embark on a house-hunting expedition it would be wise to bring along an expert.

You should not expect to find an old house in perfect condition, and if you do you can be assured that it will have a staggering price tag. Old houses will inevitably have flaws. It is possible to detect these flaws and estimate the cost of correcting them. But unless you are an architect or an engineer, you will need the help of a professional to make this kind of evaluation.

There are several ways to enlist professional help to advise you during your house hunting. Many architects will give a house a brief but knowledgeable inspection for fifty to one hundred dollars. Also, all major cities have organizations that specialize in residential inspection. They will deliver a more thorough report than most architects, but they will not be concerned with the potential the house may have or the kind of living you intend to do in it. They will simply supply you with a detailed appraisal of the house as it stands. An engineer can also give you some sound counseling: flaws that a layman might consider serious enough to rule out the purchase of a house may not seem nearly so grave to an architect or engineer who knows how they may be remedied.

THE ARCHITECT

Since you most probably will require the aid of an architect when you are actually restoring your house, your best course would be to have that same architect help you select it. He will be extremely diligent in inspecting a house that he may eventually redesign, and his services, this early in the game, can be invaluable.

An architect is a specialist in exactly the problems you are about to confront. He is your professional representative and can advise you on all matters concerning the property, and even such personal ones as financing. He will not let you forget your needs, desires, and financial capabilities, and he will see possibilities—or impossibilities—that you would not. The hunting period is also an excellent time for you to get to know your architect and for him to get to know you. The two of you will be working to create your personal environment, and the better you understand each other the more workable—and pleasurable—that environment will be. In the long run, engaging an architect may be your soundest investment, one that will save you far more than the architect's fee.

FINDING AN ARCHITECT

Not every architect, of course, is interested in remodeling a city house on a limited budget. And not every architect will share your tastes. Some architects you will like, others you will not. Obviously, it would be convenient to have a friend who is an architect and who shares your enthusiasm for the row house. In any case, architects are not difficult to find.

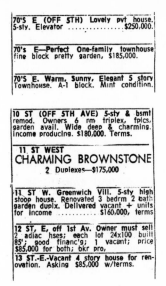

If you have friends who have renovated row houses you can consult them. You can go on tours of renovated homes, frequent in most major cities, and then contact any architect whose work you admire. Brownstone-owner associations—there are more than a hundred of these non-profit organizations in New York City alone—will gladly suggest architects whom their members have engaged. You can purchase such magazines as *House Beautiful* and *House and Home*—or visit a library and examine any of numerous architectural magazines not sold on the newsstands—and then contact any architect whose work strikes your fancy. If none of these methods turns up an architect you like, you can call the local office of the American Institute of Architects and explain your problem. The local office will usually have a committee of architects who are particularly interested in residential design and will gladly recommend a list of several.

REAL ESTATE ADS AND AGENTS

A glance at the real estate section of the newspaper will acquaint you with a lexicon of words like "charming," "spacious," "handsome," and "stately." Remember one thing: what you are reading is largely fiction. The phrase "move-in condition" may mean exactly what it says or it may mean that, armed with water, candles, and a pup tent, you could camp in the house overnight. The phrase "needs work" may mean that the walls need painting or that the house needs walls. Even those seemingly honest ads—"in terrible shape; needs loving care"—are designed to grab your attention and make you lower your guard.

Once you have compared a few real estate ads with the structures they describe you will be able to decode this rather opaque literary form and draw from it the information you need—that there is a house for sale, in the area you want, at a price you can afford to pay.

When you go to inspect a house you will be confronted with a real estate agent, the owner of the house, or both. Obviously, they do not have your best interests in mind. Their intent is to sell the house, at the best possible price. In the next chapter I have devoted a section to bargaining with real estate agents and owners.

EVALUATING A HOUSE

Buying a house is the largest single transaction most couples ever make, yet it is often guided by heated emotion rather than reason. All too frequently a prospective buyer is carried away by an ornate brass chandelier with smoky glass globes and forgets that the house around the chandelier is the wrong size or cannot be made habitable for any amount he can possibly afford.

By far the best way to evaluate a house is to rely on the judgment of a professional, your architect. However, the layman can make a fairly good estimate of the condition and desirability of a city house on his own, and consult an architect or other expert only when he thinks he has found the right house.

When you first approach the house you will get a general impression of its size, its orientation, and its facade, and will know if they fit your requirements. While you are still outside, you can examine the exterior wall. Once inside, you should first make a quick tour of the house, and then, if you are still interested, investigate the entire house from cellar to roof, carefully and slowly.

CHECKLISTS

You will look at a large number of houses, and unless you are blessed with a photographic memory it would be wise to visit each house armed with pencil and paper. Perhaps the best way to keep track of all the necessary data you will collect when you inspect a house is to devise a checklist. Have the checklist Xeroxed or copied in some other way, and take a copy wherever you go. If any of the floors has an unusual layout, you can sketch a rough plan on the back of your checklist to refresh your memory later. A camera can also be helpful when you are seeing many houses.

SIZE AND ORIENTATION

Before considering the condition of the house itself you should evaluate two important aspects of the structure that you will be unable to change—its size and orientation.

A narrow row house—between twelve and fifteen feet—is quite practical for one-family use, but would probably be cramped for two families or more. A wider house can be made into duplexes or floor-through apartments, and the rooms will probably be grander than those of a smaller structure. Tenants mean income, but they also mean less privacy and more responsibility. You may find yourself changing your mind again and again about the kind of living you want as you weigh the various factors.

Orientation—the direction a house faces—is particularly important because of the shape of the row house. It is a long narrow rectangle with windows at the short ends. Most homeowners agree that it is desirable to have the rear of the

house facing south so that the living rooms can open onto a sunny garden or terrace. Real estate agents also agree, and houses with this orientation tend to cost more. Still, there are some advantages to the opposite exposure: if the rear of the house faces north the garden will be shady and cool, and, if there are no large buildings across the street in front, the house may still be sunny and cheerful inside. A properly planted north garden can be lush and attractive, although if you are a really serious gardener, you will want a south garden. On the other hand, if you are a serious painter you will relish the opportunity of having a studio with a north exposure overlooking a garden.

Corner houses are always desirable. They offer more light and air and a feeling of extra space. Such houses are, however, more expensive, and the taxes are higher.

Facades are partly detail, such as fine bronze doors and handsome cornices, and partly the overall impression of the row. If the roof cornice is in such poor shape that it must be removed, a simple cap molding can retain the harmony of the row. Restoration of fine detail is extremely expensive, and sometimes impossible, so it is a definite advantage to find such features in perfect condition.

THE EXTERIOR WALL

The front exterior wall of a row house should be examined carefully. If the exterior wall is in need of serious repair you might well be advised to reject the house immediately. Extensive refinishing can, in some cases, be enormously expensive.

If the house you are considering is a brownstone and the brownstone is in good condition you are fortunate. Refinishing of brownstone is expensive and should be attempted only by experts. Shoddy refinishing can easily be spotted by even the novice; the new work does not match the old and the house looks piebald. If the brownstone demands extensive refinishing you can count on its costing several thousand dollars.

A brick exterior wall, on the other hand, offers few problems. At worst, the brick may have to be repointed, the joints refilled with mortar. Badly eroded mortar can leak, causing damage to the inside walls. Brick exterior walls can easily be sandblasted, although sandblasting does erode the surface of the brick. Cheaper than sandblasting, a simple cleaning can greatly improve the appearance of brick. In fact, in most cities you can rent steel stacking scaffold and clean the brick yourself. Paint can also enliven a brick exterior. Although the wall will have to be repainted every few years, a painted brick exterior can form a striking and attractive facade for your city house.

Limestone exterior walls also present few problems. They can be readily sandblasted or steam-cleaned.

Wood exteriors, now rare in eastern cities, can be restored with a few coats of paint. And if the house you are considering has an exterior wall covered with mineral shingles, you may be extremely fortunate. Under the shingles there may be clapboard, preserved in mint condition.

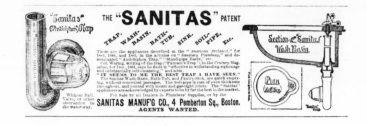
THE CELLAR

In city houses the cellar is usually completely below grade. When inspecting the cellar you should first look for high-water marks, the signs of flooding. If flooding has occurred you will definitely want to know what caused it. An unexpected catastrophe such as a ruptured water main is unlikely to recur and the flooding will not be a problem to you. Runoff from a neighbor's drainage or sewage system, or overflow from an underground stream, however, is very apt to recur and can be a serious and expensive problem. As a general rule, I would suggest that you ignore any house plagued with such flooding problems.

The sills—the heavy wood or concrete members stretching along the top of the masonry and supporting the overhead beams—should be carefully inspected. Wood sills are frequently rotted from long exposure to moisture and may have to be replaced. If the wood can be easily flaked with a screwdriver or penknife, then concrete or treated wood sills will have to be installed. Rotted sills, however, should not necessarily rule out a house. Sills can be replaced at reasonable cost. But if the moisture that caused the rot cannot be eliminated, the house should be rejected. A damp cellar will be the cause of endless problems.

Headroom is also an important factor in the cellar, especially if you plan to make use of the space for a workshop or game room. Also, while in the cellar, you should check what you can of the electrical, plumbing, and heating systems.

ELECTRICAL SYSTEM

Really evaluating the electrical system of a house is a job for an electrician, and you will be wise to have one inspect any house you are seriously considering buying. In most houses available to you, however, it is safe to say that you will need at least partial rewiring. Few old houses are wired to handle such things as air conditioners and electric kitchen appliances. To be sure, you can examine the panel board in the cellar. If there are three wires leading to the panel board, then the house is supplied with 240 volts, the voltage necessary for many modern appliances. If there are only two wires leading to the panel board, however, the house is supplied with only 120 volts and probably some rewiring will be necessary. You can also check the amperage rating, sometimes indicated on a metal disk or tag on the meter. If you intend to install air conditioners or electric kitchen appliances you will need 150-200 amperes supply.

Later, as you go through the upstairs rooms, you should notice how many outlets there are and how they are placed, whether ceiling fixtures are switch-controlled or have pullchains, and so on. Chances are that you will want much more wiring than there is, and it may not be possible to add it without replacing the whole system.

PLUMBING

If the plumbing in a house is more than twenty years old it will almost certainly not meet current code requirements and standards and will have to be replaced, bit

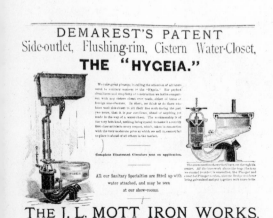

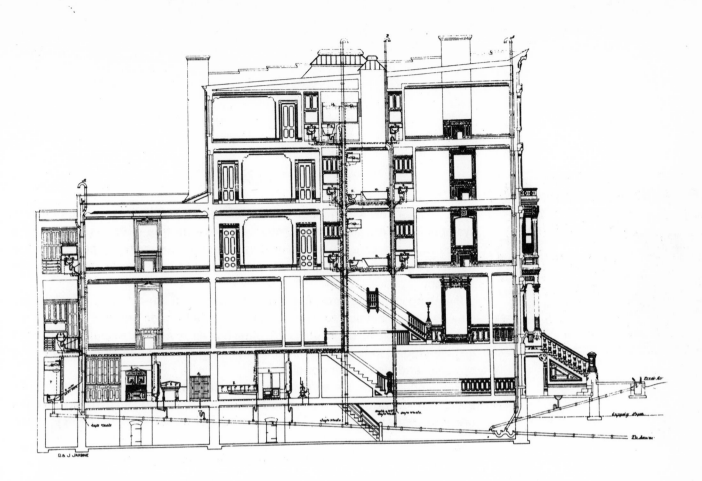

A contemporary section through a large
nineteenth-century house showing the plumbing
system, and a modern diagram. The dotted
lines in the latter are air vents; today all fixtures
must be vented.

by bit or all at once, before too long. Also, if the house has been vacant for any length of time it may have very little plumbing left. Vacant houses are frequently vandalized, and lead and brass pipes, valuable as junk, are among the first things to be pilfered.

When inspecting the plumbing in the cellar you should check the type of pipe that has been used. If the supply pipes are brass they are probably in good condition and can be retained. Galvanized iron supply lines, on the other hand, have a short life-span and will certainly have to be replaced within a few years. Drainpipes should also be carefully examined. Building codes now require heavy, thick-walled cast-iron drainpipes, but older pipes are often thin-walled and fragile, and they may be rusted nearly through. To check, tap the pipes with something made of metal. The older, thin-walled pipe will make a metallic ring, while the modern, thick-walled pipe will make a dead, stonelike clank.

You can also run your hand along the bottom of any exposed pipe in the basement to check for leakage. Leakage at any point along a horizontal run of pipe suggests that the whole run is about ready for replacement. Pipes that have been wrapped with tarpaper and wire speak for themselves. Leakage at a joint, however, is easily repaired, although it may indicate chronic blockage in the house system. If you can, you should try to trace the route of both the supply and drainpipes from the cellar through the rest of the house. This will allow you to examine the plaster in these areas for leaks.

One thing to remember is that faulty plumbing should not lead you to rule out an otherwise desirable house. In fact, bad plumbing can be a powerful tool with which to bargain. A good haggler may use it to lower the price of a house by several thousand dollars, more than enough to pay for a new system, installed exactly to his specifications.

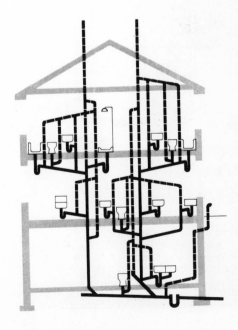

Sanitary Appliances.

Original ironwork grills are decorative even if the heating system no longer requires them. Tin ceilings are something else. They may have been put in over good plaster simply because they were in fashion, or they may cover severe damage—the renovator must take his chances.

HEATING

Most houses you will inspect will contain either hot-water or steam heating systems. Both are economical, relatively problem-free methods of heating a house. Such systems can vary considerably—one-pipe and two-pipe systems are the most common—and should be evaluated by an engineer or knowledgeable architect.

If you are fortunate enough to find a house with a hot-air heating system you may be able to convert to central heating and air conditioning at minimum expense. Although the ducts utilized in older hot-air systems are smaller than those installed today, they may be adequate for most modern gas or electric heating systems, and also for air conditioning.

Remember to ask the owner or broker about the cost of heating the house using the existing system if you intend to keep it. It is a good idea to ask to see the previous year's bills from the utilities company to be certain of the heating costs.

INTERIOR WALLS AND CEILINGS

After you leave the cellar you will want to inspect the interior walls and ceilings of every room in the house. Gaping cracks or fissures that run *diagonally* near doors or windows or across the ceilings are signs that the house suffers from some structural weakness that must be corrected. Some sort of structural reinforcement such as shoring or bracing will be needed. These repairs can be inexpensive or costly, depending on the work required. Again, an architect or engineer can be invaluable in estimating the costs of such repairs.

Smaller cracks, running *horizontally* or *vertically,* are routine, however—the common symptoms of a house experiencing old age. They are apt to recur a few months after patching or painting, and unless you want to replaster completely must be accepted as the legacy of the house. In some old houses, moreover, you are likely to find that a combination of vibration, moisture, and old age has caused the plaster to separate from the lath, causing unsightly sags and lumps. This condition, although it demands replastering, should not prevent you from buying an otherwise sound house.

One word of warning to apartment dwellers: Do not overlook hallways and their ceilings. You will be surprised at how much wall and ceiling space exists in the halls of a city house. A friend with a rather small row house recently discovered that it took eight gallons of paint merely to prime these areas.

MOLDINGS AND INTRICATE PLASTERWORK

One of the most charming features of old city houses is the intricate plasterwork often found in ceilings and cornices. If you find a house with this plasterwork intact you will have uncovered a treasure. But if, as is the case in most old city houses, the moldings are damaged or missing, there are still several alternatives open to you.

Restoration is one, but it is costly. Large simplified items such as corbels and heavy moldings can be replaced at moderate cost, but intricately carved, detailed plasterwork is grossly expensive to restore if it can be restored at all. Another alternative is to rip out the plasterwork, replaster, and think of the money you saved. A third alternative is to treat this damaged plasterwork as attractive ruin and leave it unpainted in an otherwise freshly painted room. One enterprising homeowner who employed this technique plans to restore his cornice at a later date, after he has made a mold and cast the twenty lacking corbels himself.

WINDOWS

Curiously enough an old house will often be rejected because its windows are badly in need of repair. Yet windows can easily be replaced at reasonable cost. Many woodworking shops are geared to make individual window sash to precise measurements, and simple sash (one pane over one pane) with frame and sill can be built and installed for less than one hundred dollars each. Complicated windows are more costly, but, all things considered, a few hundred dollars can replace all the windows. And new windows mean a more weathertight house and therefore lower heating costs.

FLOORS

Badly sagging floors may be a sign of weakness in the floor joists, a structural flaw that can be expensive to repair. If you find a sagging floor, check the ceiling below. If the ceiling has not sagged and is in good condition, then the installation of new flooring may solve the problem. If the ceiling below also sags, however, new joists will probably be required. Although installing new floor joists can be costly, they should not entirely rule out an otherwise attractive house.

Also check the floor surfaces. Early in the history of these old houses, parquet was often added over the pine flooring. It may look grimy, but sanding may reveal a stunning intricate inlay of varicolored hardwoods, usually set in an elaborate geometric border design. Strip hardwood floors can also be sanded. Sanding machines can be rented from hardware stores, but they are extremely heavy; it is probably worth paying a professional to do the sanding. Pine floors can also be sanded, and the novice will have an easier time with them. Results are quicker, and the result is most impressive.

THE ROOF

Evaluating the roof is mainly a matter of carefully checking the ceiling of the top floor. Any evidence of water stains or flaking or sagging plaster is a clear indication that a new roof is in order. A walk on the roof is also advised. Large bubbles in the roofing mean that moisture has seeped under the surface, and the need for a new roof is imminent. Roofing is not expensive, as long as the planking under the roofing is in fairly good shape, but repairing old damage in the rooms below can be messy and costly.

Drainage of water from the roof is important. Old houses may have outside or inside leaders, and either is acceptable. Interior leaders, however, are more practical, since there is less concern with freezing during the winter months, and there is less exposure of the leaders to the elements. Your architect can inspect the drainage system, tell you if it will have to be replaced, and estimate the cost.

While on the roof you will have a chance to inspect the chimneys to see if they are open and appear operable. A closed chimney is not a danger sign. In most cases the chimneys were blocked up merely to eliminate the need for maintenance when central heating was installed and the fireplaces were no longer the main source of warmth.

FIREPLACES

If you have found the chimneys open you can check the fireplaces on your way back down through the house. If you find one open, light a small piece of paper to see if the smoke is drawn up the chimney. If it is, you have a working fireplace—though usually you will be required to install new flue linings at a cost of as much as a thousand dollars per flue.

In some instances the old flues may have been blocked just to close them off after adequate central heating obviated the original need. At the time, the owner was most likely delighted to close that chapter in his life; he no longer had to keep the fireplaces going day and night. The major chimney problem in old houses is that the old brick flues were not straight and also in most cases the old mortar has turned to dust. The chimney may stand there, but it may not be altogether adequate to withstand heat and contain smoke. Hence the general requirement to install new flue linings. The fireplace itself will need to be relined with firebrick.

Opening up a blocked fireplace can be a traumatic and dirty experience. If you find all the fireplaces closed up and the flues blocked, you had better be very sure you want a fireplace before you get involved in the messy and expensive job of restoring one.

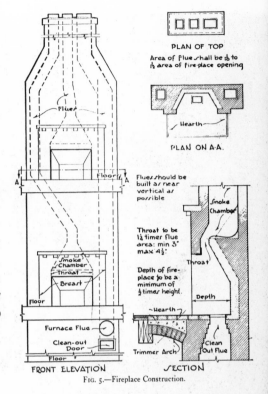

Fig. 5.—Fireplace Construction.

STAIRCASES

A badly sagging staircase is also not sufficient reason to shy away from an old house. The staircase can often be strengthened by replacing the risers, beginning at the lowest step. This type of repair is expensive but not prohibitive. Broken balusters should in no case rule out a house. Most woodworking shops can replace balusters at reasonable cost.

Most nineteenth-century houses have simple straight runs of stairs. In a house recently being remodeled, we were pleasantly surprised to find a stair which had an easier gradient and was wider than most. This must have come about as a result of the house's being built 21 feet wide and 40 feet deep—a bit wider and deeper than most. The result is remarkably noticeable—so much so that the owner has located the kitchen and dining room on the floor above the parlor so as not to disturb the feeling of the existing front and rear parlors.

A pleasant idea used extensively within duplex or triplex apartments is the spiral stair. These are available in designs for do-it-yourself. Also available are fine cast-iron spiral stairs removed from earlier installations—libraries and theaters. They may fit your location. Most ironwork shops have purchased one or two in the past. Don't hesitate to ask if it is what you want; the ironworkers seem to be a large fraternity, and can turn many dreams into reality. So when evaluating the stairs in a house, you can also consider locations for future stairs.

A well-designed garden in Greenwich Village,
both balanced and usable. The single center path
is wide enough to be used as a terrace.

The city back yard has many limitations, as can be seen in this winter view, but in summer these are surprisingly lush. The facade below is an exuberance of greenery, but vines are not good for the structure and are best treated as annuals.

BACK YARDS AND FRONT YARDS

You can't expect to move right in to a beautifully landscaped city house, but you will at least be able to get some impression of what you might be able to create. Most city houses under consideration won't have large front yards, but they should be capable of development to present a good public image. If there is any earth it can be put to good use with plants that are easy to maintain and pleasant to view. Of course the admiring public will pick your flowers, but not if they are slightly out of reach. Hardy evergreens will do very nicely in most city front yards. Consider breaking up a concrete slab to create a spot for a spruce tree which you can cover with lights at Christmas time. You'll be surprised how quickly the neighborhood adapts to that tradition.

Back yards are as wide as the lot and usually fifty or more feet deep. This is an awkward proportion, so long and narrow, but it can be enormously improved if you can convince your neighbors to eliminate fencing. This common landscaping is most famous in Turtle Bay—perhaps the first urban breakthrough in any communal way of life.

LEGAL STATUS AND TENANTS

Two important aspects of the house you buy are the legal status of the building and whether or not the building will be sold vacant. An occupied, rent-controlled building is worth considerably less money than a vacant one. Vague statements that it will only cost a few hundred dollars to vacate the building can be true, but experience has proved many times that much more is involved in time and effort; general responsibility with generally irresponsible tenants can be very discouraging. Various avenues of approach are available to defeat the remaining tenants—none of them savory. The techniques multiply and depend entirely on the weaknesses involved.

Often a house has been classed as a rooming house. If it is emptied and remodeled over a period of six months, the rooming-house classification will no longer be valid. In any case a new certificate of occupancy will be required.

Another consideration, affecting both costs and the legal status of your house, is whether to have a one- or two-family house, or a house with three or more units. The increased rentals gained from providing three or more dwelling units may well be offset by the increased costs and responsibilities. A house with three or more units is a legal multiple dwelling and requires one-hour-fire-resistant materials in the stairwell and sprinklers (anathema to brownstoners who respect the old moldings that are usually destroyed in this process). Inspections multiply and restrictions increase over the one- or two-family house. Maintenance becomes more complicated; if you are doing the work yourself you will literally become the janitor. On the other hand the income is considerably increased: four apartments return more than twice as much as two apartments in the same space.

SHOULD YOU BUY IT?

After you have looked at a large number of city houses you will begin to realize that, in many cases, a $25,000 house is considerably cheaper than a $20,000 house. You may also find that the house that most strikes your fancy and fits your pocketbook is not the house that most fits your needs.

But finally there is a decision to be made—to buy or not to buy. Your architect, your friends, your relatives, and your business associates will all give you advice, much of it sound, but the decision is yours alone.

FOUR | THE COST OF A CITY HOUSE

While looking for a house in the city may be the most enjoyable part of becoming an urban homeowner, paying for that house is certainly the bleakest part of the process, especially today when money is tight and costs are rising. When considering the purchase of a city house, or even part of a city house, you must be realistic about your purchasing potential. Know how much money you have available, both in cash and in mortgage power. Overextension can easily lead to disaster.

In this chapter I have tried to outline what costs and financial problems you can expect when you finally decide to purchase and renovate a row house, and to give you some tips that should make the process a little less painful.

The house on the facing page is still undergoing a slow, careful renovation within the budget of its owners. They are doing much of the work themselves. The row on this page in Park Slope, Brooklyn, was remodeled with private foundation funds into low-cost rental units. The challenge to retain the original character of the buildings was met.

ALTERNATIVES: CO-OPS AND CONDOMINIUMS

If you find that you cannot afford the costs of a one-family house or that you do not actually require the space, there are still two alternatives open to you—co-ops and condominiums. Both offer many of the benefits of row-house living, at a substantial cut in cost.

In a co-op you buy shares of stock in the corporation that owns the building, or group of buildings, and the land. You then execute and receive a proprietary lease on your apartment—a studio, a duplex, or even a triplex. You pay a monthly carrying charge that covers your proportionate share of the taxes, mortgage, insurance, and maintenance costs.

One good example of a row-house co-op is a complex known as 9-G, a block of nine brownstones on West 93rd Street between Central Park West and Columbus Avenue in New York City. The nine brownstones are divided into thirty-one residence units, each family or resident owning shares in the corporation. The space in 9-G is divided into half-floor units; the smallest apartment consists of two units, the largest of five. The corporation has installed a central elevator, and the back yard, basement, a dark room, and a meeting hall are communal property.

RENTING VS. OWNING

Cost of renting apartment (four or five rooms)		Cost of buying house (two-family)	
Rent	$160	Price of house	$22,500
Security	160	FHA mortgage	21,900
Commission	160	cash needed	$600
total	$480		

After ten years you have paid out 160 x12x10 = $19,200, and you have saved nothing.	After ten years you have paid off about $5000 of the mortgage.

Monthly cost		Monthly cost	
Rent	$160	Mortgage payment	$170
		Taxes	40
		Heat	30
		Insurance	10
		Maintenance	10
		total	$260
		Less rental for one apartment	$160
		net cost	$100

After twenty-five years you have paid out $48,000, and you continue to pay.	After twenty-five years the mortgage is paid off and there is a net profit each month of $70.

When you buy a house you will need several hundred dollars more to cover closing costs, and the house may need additional investment before it can earn rental income. Your lawyer or your tax accountant can help you work out a detailed summary of your expenses; it will certainly be more complicated than the simplified case shown here, but the long-term advantages of buying may be just as great or greater.

Although co-ops seem to be effective for large buildings, or complexes of renovated row houses, they might be cumbersome for a single row house. The cost alone would probably be prohibitive. 9-G, for example, was bought and renovated at a total cost well over a million dollars. And there are other drawbacks to a co-op. While you may borrow money on your apartment as a personal loan, with the shares of stock as collateral, you may not mortgage the property. Also, if you want to sell, lease, or sublet your apartment, you may do so only with the approval of the board of directors.

In a condominium, however, you purchase the apartment outright, and may acquire a mortgage that covers only your apartment. You pay only the taxes and insurance fees on your own apartment. You may sell, lease, or sublet without the consent of your neighbors. The land and such things as hallways, cellars, exteriors, and boilers are commonly owned by all tenants. You are not responsible for the legal or financial troubles of any of your neighbors, except that you may have to pay a prorated share of any default in maintenance. You may not be able to make structural changes in the apartment, but this is a common-sense rule for property protection. You may buy into an existing condominium, or band together with friends and purchase your own building.

Condominiums are one of the oldest forms of city-house ownership, dating back to ancient Rome. They are common in many Latin countries, notably Puerto Rico, where a large percentage of the existing homes are owned as condominiums. They are only beginning to appear in this country, but they should enjoy considerable success as land values rise.

BARGAINING

Although the house you buy will be owned by a person like yourself or perhaps by a corporation, you will most likely transact your business through a real estate agent. The agent is much like the used-car salesman: he may be honest but there is no reason to expect him to be. There are some 500,000 real estate brokers in the United States, and some of them are certainly conscientious, particularly in small towns and rural areas where their livelihood depends partly on goodwill. But the field of big-city real estate has attracted a host of fast talkers and shrewd operators.

Remember that the agent's primary function is not to find a house that suits you, but to find a buyer for a house he already has on his list. He is working for the seller and himself, not for you. In that respect he is the enemy—his interests are directly opposed to yours. Also remember that there is no such thing as a *bargain* when dealing with an agent. He is a professional who knows the market and whose income is dependent on the sale of his houses. He will not be asking for less than he thinks he can get.

When the agent does in fact come up with that perfect house, the house exactly right for you, try not to show it. A great deal of money is involved, and the owner of the house is just as anxious to do well by the deal as you are. If you glow with enthusiasm, you may find that the owner, "the day before," has raised the asking price. If you show your best poker face and don't allow yourself to be rushed into making a bid, the owner may lower the price. The agent, like any

— Chas Graham and Sons. ARCHTS. —

good salesman, will be reading your reactions, and if he suspects you are hooked he will certainly advise the owner not to be talked down.

Even if you are sure that the house is the one for you, you should not be hasty. The agent, if he senses your interest, will advise you to act fast. But don't be rushed. There is a small chance the house will be sold while you are making up your mind—a *small* chance.

Take time to check the agent's record with the Better Business Bureau. It is also a good idea to see if the house is handled by more than one broker. Some houses are listed by several brokers: if an agent knows you are in contact with his competition he will be more than willing to try to talk the owner down for you so that he can make the sale.

Just because of his position, however, an agent can be valuable to you. Besides helping you find a house, he can also help you find a mortgage— perhaps negotiate one himself, in fact—and he can give you vital information about such cloudy issues as contracts of sale, title searches, and closings.

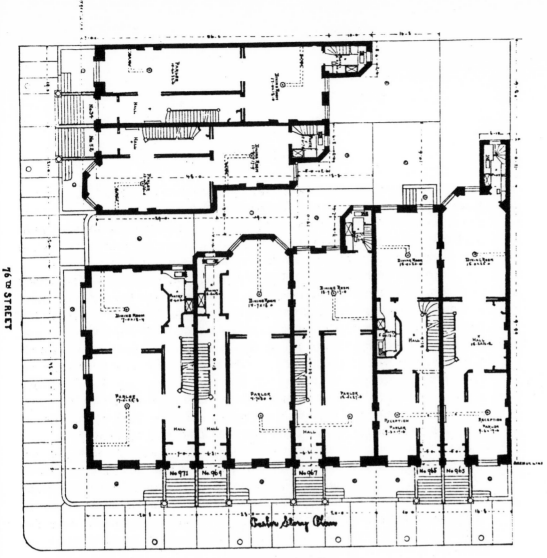

76TH STREET

MADISON AVENUE

The Seven Houses shown on Diagram, and Perspective Elevation, (see pages 11 and 12), are located on Southeast Corner of Madison Avenue and 76th Street. They are all Four Story and Basement, Brick and Brown Stone Fronts, ranging in width from 16 feet to 26 feet 8 inches. Built on solid rock foundations. They will be completed about February 1st, 1886. A Careful Inspection invited during Construction.

PRICES.

No. 963 Madison Avenue is 16 feet 8 inches wide, 65 feet 6 inches deep, with Butler's Pantry Extension additional ....   **PRICE $36,000**

No. 965 Madison Avenue is 16 feet wide, 61 feet 6 inches deep ....   **PRICE $34,000**

No. 967 Madison Avenue is 20 feet wide, 51 feet 6 inches deep, with Butler's Pantry Extension additional ....   **PRICE $37,000**

No. 969 Madison Avenue is 23 feet wide, 55 feet deep ....   **PRICE $40,000**

No. 971 Madison Avenue (Corner House), is 26 feet 8 inches wide, 48 feet deep..   **PRICE $48,000**

No. 32 East 76th Street is 21 feet wide, 56 feet deep, with Butler's Pantry Extension carried to Fourth Story ....   **PRICE $35,000**

No. 34 East 76th Street is 19 feet wide, 56 feet deep, with Butler's Pantry Extension additional...........................   **PRICE $35,000**

☞ The Plumbing, Drainage and Ventilation of all our Houses arranged and executed according to the latest requirements of Sanitary Science.

DESCRIPTION OF THE CONSTRUCTION AND FINISH OF OUR HOUSES.

PLUMBING AND DRAINAGE.

The very best workmanship and materials throughout, according to the latest requirements of Sanitary Science.

WARMING AND COOKING APPARATUS.

Each House will have a Moist Warm Air Furnace (with Automatic Water Supply) set in brick chamber; heat will be carried to all extensions, bath rooms, and up to fourth floor. The Mansion, No. 23 West 57th Street, will be Steam Heated throughout, with the latest improved system of indirect Radiation.

ALL KITCHENS will be supplied with French wrought iron ranges, with metal hoods, checks, and plate warming shelves. A separate vent flue built in walls over each range to carry off smoke and smell, arising from cooking. Separate Laundry Ranges in Dining Room Extension Houses.

VENTILATING OF CEILINGS.

A separate vent carried to roof over gas outlets of large rooms.

MIRRORS.

Each House will have Handsome Plate Glass Mirrors over parlor and second story mantels. Also Plate Glass Mirrors over wash basins. Handsome Cabinet Hall Stand, with Mirror, in main front halls.

CABINET WORK.

Parlors, main halls, including front and vestibule doors, and first flight of stairs, will be trimmed and finished in handsome Mahogany or Cherry. Dining Rooms trimmed in quartered Oak. Stairs Hard-wood throughout.

SECOND STORIES.

All second stories trimmed in Hard-wood; inside Hard-wood blinds on fronts from basement to fourth story. All this work executed and finished cabinet style.

MANTELS, GRATES, FENDERS AND HEARTHS.

All mantels Hard-wood throughout. Furnished with Handsome Hearths, Fire Places, Grates and Fenders of the Latest Designs.

FLOORS.

All Floors double deafened with Building Felt between each Floor.

SIDEWALKS AND CEMENT WORK.

Sidewalks laid with single flagstone from area coping to curb. Areas, Yards and Cellars carefully Cemented and drained.

THE CONTRACT OF SALE

Once you have finally selected a house to buy, at a price you can afford, you then enter into a written contract of sale or binder with the seller. Under no conditions should you sign a contract of sale or binder, or make a deposit of any kind, without the approval of a qualified attorney. Your rights are governed solely by the document, and you should be aware of what you are getting into.

Invariably, you will pay a deposit upon signing the contract of sale or binder, usually 10 percent of the purchase price. Before you make this deposit a good attorney will demand proof of the seller's identity, or certification by a reputable attorney. He will determine whether the property described in the contract of sale is actually the property you are buying. He will also check to see if there are such things as party-wall agreements on record. Such an agreement, for example, could prohibit you from increasing the height of the building. Moreover, your attorney will require that the deposit be held in escrow by the seller's attorney, so that it may be returned if the sale is not completed. If the deposit is not held in escrow, it could be spent before the sale was completely negotiated.

A word of warning: do not, under any condition, begin work on the house until after the closing, which will, if all goes well, occur a few weeks after you have signed the contract of sale. Even if you are on the best of terms with the seller and the broker, remember that a contract of sale does not mean you own the house. Any number of things could go wrong—the seller may not have clear title to the house, or mortgages may not be available—and the transaction can be called off. Any money or time you have spent on the house will then have gone for nothing. If you have enthusiastically rushed in and ripped down a wall, you may be in an embarrassing position.

TITLE SEARCH AND INSURANCE

After the contract of sale has been signed, your attorney will initiate a title search. This search, which usually takes from three to four weeks, is carried out by a title company. It assures you that the seller has a clear title to the property, and that there are no liens on the docket. Most mortgage lenders also require a title-insurance policy. These policies are issued by the title company and are a wise and fairly inexpensive investment. A title search and title-insurance policy on a $50,000 brownstone in New York City, for example, would cost about $300. This fee covers the title during the entire time you own the property.

THE CLOSING

The closing, the final step in actually taking ownership of your house, can be a harrowing experience. A large amount of your money changes hands, and you will be dealing with people you have never met who communicate in a legal language you will probably not understand. And the crowd can be large, including you, the sellers, the broker, an attorney for everyone concerned (five or six lawyers at a closing is not uncommon), and a representative of the mortgage holder. Being an architect, I have attended several closings, yet I was astonished at how overpowering it all became when it was my money and my house involved.

You should go to the closing prepared to write checks in excess of anything you had expected. Besides the down payment, there are a host of closing costs—taxes, escrow money, insurance, the legal fee for the mortgage lender's lawyer, and innumerable odds and ends—and there is nothing for you to do but pay them. If, for example, the seller has made mortgage payments, or paid utilities or tax bills since the contract of sale, there will have to be an adjustment made and again you must pay.

There is no way around closing costs. If a broker advertises "No closing costs," as is frequently done in the suburbs, do not be misled. The costs will be included in the price of the house.

MORTGAGES

Few people buy city houses today by simply writing a check for the purchase amount. Most of us carry mortgages. And with money tight and real estate and construction costs rising at about 5 percent a year, mortgages for city houses are becoming harder and harder to obtain.

In neighborhoods where row houses are still reasonably priced, financial assistance is especially hard to get. Ironically, the worst offenders are the great savings banks, housed in Greek or Roman temples and decked with beautiful white marble and perfect egg-and-dart moldings. Such banks physically dominate most decaying neighborhoods. Realizing that there are better investments in "safer" neighborhoods, these banks have held tightly to their money. Only recently, thanks to severe media criticism, has at least token funding been carried out.

Before you purchase a house, you should be well aware of your mortgage potential. Here the real estate agent can be of great help to you. He can lead you toward a decent mortgage—he'll have to in order to make his sale. Also you can consult your lawyer and any homeowners' association in your future neighborhood about mortgage possibilities.

Contrary to the American tradition against indebtedness, which would suggest that you make as large a down payment as possible in order to reduce monthly payments, in most cases you would be wise to put down only a minimum down payment, even though it will reduce your equity and raise your monthly costs. For one thing, you may need all your available cash for renovation. Also, assuming that prices continue to rise, you will be paying off your mortgage with money at an increasingly lower value. The interest rate on most mortgages never changes, but you should be careful here. More and more, as money becomes tighter, mortgages contain clauses that allow for adjustable interest rates.

Balloon Mortgages. The balloon mortgage is a relatively new type of loan, especially applicable to city houses. Most mortgage lenders will not instigate a loan on a row house until the renovation has been completed and a certificate of occupancy obtained. And even then you may not be able to acquire a regular mortgage for some time. The balloon mortgage is, in a sense, a preamble to the regular mortgage; it allows you to go on with the renovation and search for a regular mortgage.

There are, however, dangers in the balloon mortgage. The mortgage only covers a period of from six months to five years. During this time the payments and interest are usually reasonable, but at the end of the period the balance of the mortgage must be paid, in a lump sum. Sometimes, while remodeling is still in progress or before a regular mortgage has been obtained, the balloon mortgage comes due and the impoverished owner is forced to sell at a loss. It is an infrequent but possible occurrence.

Conventional Mortgages. The majority of house mortgages are known as conventional mortgages as opposed to government-insured VA and FHA mortgages. They are made by private lenders such as banks, savings and loan associations, insurance companies, and mortgage brokers. A conventional mortgage can also be obtained from a friend, a relative, or a business associate.

The down payment, maximum repayment period, closing cost charges, and contract clauses can all vary in the conventional mortgage. There is no uniformity requirement, so you should be aware of any special features in your mortgage. Your attorney can decode the fine print for you.

VA Mortgages. The Veterans Administration mortgage or GI mortgage is only available to veterans of World War II or the Korean War, although you may take over a VA mortgage if you purchase a house from a veteran. There are two sources for such a loan, the VA itself or a private lender such as a bank or insurance company. The VA insures this lender against loss should you default.

The VA mortgage offers a low down payment and low interest rates, but unfortunately, as money becomes tight and lenders can make better investments elsewhere, such mortgages become difficult if not impossible to obtain. If you are a veteran you can inquire at your local VA office to see if mortgages are available and under what terms.

FHA Mortgages. The Federal Housing Administration's mortgage program services both veterans and non-veterans, although veterans and servicemen are offered special terms. Like the VA mortgage, the FHA mortgage allows you to buy a house for a small down payment at small interest rates. FHA mortgages, however, can only be obtained from private lenders. The FHA insures these lenders against default.

POINTS

The mortgage rate you pay to a bank or mortgage lender is fixed by law. Many banks and mortgage lenders, however, require that you pay "points" before a mortgage will be given. One point is equal to 1 percent of the purchase price of the house, and sometimes as many as fourteen points are charged.

Points are sometimes referred to as bonuses; they are really amounts of money paid to the mortgagee as an inducement to lend the mortgagor the money. Points have become common practice in the banking world in the past three or four years. The points are usually subtracted from the amount of the loan. For example, on a $40,000 mortgage with four points, you receive $38,400 and repay $40,000. Legal restrictions on rates of interest are generally responsible for this widespread practice. Fortunately, points, being a decidedly negative element, are negotiable, so it is recommended that efforts be made to shop around for the most favorable set of charges. They are not all the same.

MY OWN HOUSE

The first house I decided to buy was a charming red brick Victorian in Brooklyn that was selling for about $28,000 with a $6,000 down payment. When I signed the contract of sale and made the necessary deposit, I was wide-eyed and enthusiastic. It was a show of emotion I was soon to regret.

Between the contract of sale and the date set for the closing, I discovered that a mortgage was virtually impossible to get, even though one of the sellers was himself a mortgage broker. The sellers, it seems, had realized that the house was more valuable than they had suspected. Claiming that financing the house had become overly complicated, the sellers raised the down payment considerably. After careful deliberation, I decided that the increased down payment made the house considerably less appealing, low cash outlay being one of the major advantages of buying an old city house, and I called off the transaction. My deposit was refunded and again I set out to find a house. (Had I begun work on the house when I signed the contract of sale, the money spent would have been wasted. I did, in fact, draw up plans for the renovation, labor that was altogether useless.)

I looked at several other houses in the same neighborhood and soon found one I liked—the house I now own.

The house, one of a row of identical red brick four-story houses with high stoops, had been recently purchased by the sellers at auction from the city for $17,000. They added new roofing, painted the interior, made a few minor repairs, and then put the house up for sale for $25,000, with a down payment of $6,000. Bargaining brought the down payment down to $5,000, and I purchased the house.

There was an existing mortgage on the house, which I took over. The mortgage, amounting to about $12,000 at 6 percent and extending over a fifteen-year period, was held by the City of New York. To cover the rest of the purchase price,

My own house, and some of the documents prepared by my conscientious lawyer. I went to great lengths to preserve the fine brick: several layers of yellow paint were removed by hand with paint remover. The effect is a soft blending of natural colors. Sandblasting would have been much quicker but the hard surface of the Philadelphia brick would have been lost. The brownstone trim has been painted with black masonry paint to emphasize the contrast.

HARRY MITCHELL
COUNSELLOR AT LAW
4607 FORT HAMILTON PARKWAY
BROOKLYN, N. Y. 11219
GEdney 8-6666

April 2, 1968.

Mr. H. Dickson McKenna
425 East 70th Street
New York, New York

Dear Mr. McKenna:

I have made a rough estimate of the money you will need at the Closing of Title. I suggest that you bring a total of $5,300.00 in the following form: certified check or checks to your own order for $4,300.00 and either cash or half a dozen ordinary checks to take care of approximately $1,000.00.

My estimate is based on the following:

Price	$25,000.00
Fee to Seller's attorney for drawing bond and mortgage	50.00
Insurance premium	100.00
Taxes	125.00
Water and Sewer	57.00
Escrow to new mortgagees for taxes, water and sewer	75.00
Fee to me	250.00
Total	$25,657.00

From this total there are to be deducted the following credits:

Deposit	$ 2,500.00
New York City mortgage	11,020.00
Second mortgage	7,200.00
	$20,720.00

	$25,657.00
	20,720.00
Estimated balance due at Closing	$ 4,937.00

Cordially yours,

Harry Mitchell

HM:mlm   HARRY MITCHELL

the seller then took back a balloon mortgage amounting to about $8,000. This mortgage was also at 6 percent and covers a five-year period. At the end of that time, the balance, about $5,000, must be paid in cash.

Renovating the house cost another $25,000. I obtained the money for this work from a bank, in the form of a personal loan, using stock as collateral. I then discovered—too late, unfortunately—that since the house is located in an urban renewal area the renovation could have been financed at a considerably lower rate of interest.

When the second mortgage is due I plan to obtain a mortgage of approximately 80 percent of the market value of the house, estimated to be about $70,000 at that date. The current rate of interest on mortgages at this time will influence this decision, but the financing on the house would justify the mortgage.

I estimate the income on my house to be $700 per month, a figure that includes not only the rent from the basement apartment but an estimate of what I should charge myself for rent. Most owners make the mistake of assuming they live rent-free in their houses. To calculate the income of a city house properly you must consider the space you yourself occupy, since otherwise it could be supplying you with income. Your own rent is the money you lose by not renting to someone else.

Admittedly I made some minor mistakes in buying and renovating the house—everybody does. Before the renovation began, for example, I engaged a demolition contractor to take down a ceiling and one wall. Had I waited until the renovation had begun, I might have been able to salvage some materials from the demolition and perhaps have saved several hundred dollars. Also, while an electrician was rewiring the house, I innocently asked for outlets not listed in the job specification. When I received the bill I discovered that these outlets cost me a staggering $800 over the original price of the rewiring. Despite this, I am genuinely pleased with the house I own, and consider it a sound investment.

Robert H. Fuller, Esq.
AT OFFICE OF 16 Court Street, Brooklyn, N. Y.

STATEMENT ON CLOSING TITLE to and Memorandum of mortgages on premises, No. 546 State Street,

Brooklyn, New York, the 3rd day of April 19 68

East Realty and others, Seller to H. Dickson McKenna, Buyer

All adjustments as of April 3, 19 68

CREDIT BUYER			DEBIT BUYER		
Paid on Contract	$ 2,500	00	Purchase Price	$25,000	00
			Insurance Liab.	63	38
Mortgage held by The City of NY	11,158	00			
Int. from 1/1/68 @ 6 % 3/31/68 d	167	38			
2nd Mortgage Int. to 4/3/68	3	66			
Int. from @ % m d			Rent from to		
3rd Mortgage					
Int. from @ % m d					
Purchase money mortgage to Sellers	7,200	00			
			Taxes as adjusted @ $255.70 ½ 1967/68 2nd half Closing to 6/30/68	126	02
Rent from to					
			Water as adjusted @ $69. yr., Closing to 12/31/68	51	32
Security on lease			Sewer @ $23 yr. Closing to 6/30/68	5	51
			Fuel		
Taxes as adjusted					
Water as adjusted					
Assessments			TOTAL DEBIT	$25,246	23
			TOTAL CREDIT, brought over	21,029	04
			BALANCE PAID TO SELLER	$ 4,217	19
TOTAL CREDIT	$21,029	04			
			Disbursements by Seller		
			Revenue Stamps		
Disbursements by Buyer			Drawing Papers		
			Recording Papers		

April 5, 1968.

Mr. H. Dickson McKenna
425 East 70th Street
New York, New York

Re: Purchase of 546 State Street, Brooklyn

Dear Mr. McKenna:

This Summary and the attached Settlement Figures constitute my report of the Closing of Title.

PRESENT AT THE CLOSING WERE:

George Harkavy - President of Wilmikwil Corp. - Seller
Gladys S. Guile - Seller
Messrs. Gallant, Wollens, Sternklar - Partners, East Realty - Seller
H. Dickson McKenna - Buyer
Harry Mitchell - Attorney for Buyer
Robert H. Fuller - Attorney for Sellers
Samuel Muchnick for Chicago Title Insurance Company
James Coyle for Beacon Heights, Ltd. - Broker

PAPERS DELIVERED AT THE CLOSING WERE:

Deed Sellers to Buyer (TRB) ( )
Purchase Money Mortgage Note from Buyer to Sellers (S) (CHM)
Purchase Money Mortgage (TRS) (CHM)
Copy of First Mortgage of 1967 (HM)
Liability policy (E)
City Real Estate Transfer Tax Return (TFC)
Title Company bill and receipt (HM)

KEY TO LETTERS IN PARENTHESES ABOVE:

CHM - Copy held by me subject to your request
E - Enclosed herewith
HM - Held by me subject to your request
TFC - Taken by title company to be filed with the City of N. Y.
TRB - Taken by title company to be recorded and sent to you via my office
TRS - Taken by title company to be recorded and sent to the Sellers

Net due Sellers, after adjustments, was $4,217.19.
This you paid by bank check $4,300.00
Excess returned   82.81*
                                   $4,217.19

*The excess was returned by:
Sellers' check to Robert H. Fuller,
approved by you $50.00
Sellers' check to you   32.81
                                    $82.81

Expenses Paid by Buyer:
Chicago Title Insurance Company $233.00
  Examination Fee $172.00
  Department Searches   10.00
  Mortgage Tax   36.00
  Recording Deed   6.50
  Mortgage   8.50
                             $233.00
This you paid by your check.

Robert H. Fuller:
Fee for drawing Purchase Money Note and Mortgage,
by return check of Sellers a/c of excess paid
by you above purchase price $50.00
You also paid at Closing for principal and interest
on first mortgage (held by City), applied to interest from 1/1/68 to 3/31/68 $167.38*
a/c principal   144.62*
                                     $312.00

*After this payment your first mortgage balance is $11,013.38.

Although you will be paying a monthly escrow sum to the second mortgagees and they in turn will be paying for you the principal and interest on the first mortgage, taxes, water and sewer charges, the bills from the City will be coming to you. When you receive the bills you should note the contents and then forward the bills to the second mortgagees for payment.

At the Closing you paid to the second mortgagees $180.00 to establish the escrow fund. I suggest that you keep a separate record of the deposits you make to the escrow fund as well as the payments made by the second mortgagee out of the escrow fund. In the future, your monthly escrow payments will be $155.00. This monthly figure is subject to change as taxes, water and sewer charges are changed.

Your total monthly payment to the second mortgagees starting May 3, 1968 will be $227.00.
This total will be made up of the following:
For principal and interest $ 72.00
For escrow fund   155.00
                                    $227.00

I suggest that on the back of each monthly check you show the breakdown for principal and interest $72.00 and for escrow $155.00. Your monthly payments should be made to Helen Wollens and Lila Sternklar, c/o Sternklar, 1619 51st Street, Brooklyn, New York.

I will obtain and send to you a second mortgage chart detailing the allocations of principal and interest out of each monthly payment of $72.00. This will not be necessary as far as the first mortgage is concerned because the City sends you monthly bills which contain such details.

The purchase money mortgage allows you to "proceed and complete any legal renovations."

When the title policy comes in, I will send it to you.

As a result of the payments made at the Closing, your taxes are paid to June 30, 1967. Your water is paid to December 31, 1968 and your sewer charges are paid to June 30, 1968.

Liability policy GL 61677 Investors of America (Jack Stahl, broker, 229 Beach 125th Street, Rockaway Park, New York) was turned over to you by the Sellers. You telephoned Mr. Stahl and arranged for endorsement of your name on the policy.

You also called your own broker and ordered fire policy Aetna Casualty 73 FP 919227 for $35,000.00. The second mortgagees are entitled to receive the original policy under the terms of the mortgage. When you receive the policy, I suggest that you send the original to the mortgagees.

In a parallel transaction, the purchase money mortgage was assigned by the Sellers to Helen Wollers and Lila Sternklar.

Best of luck to you in your new property.

Cordially yours,

HARRY MITCHELL

HM:mlm
encl

113

FIVE | RENOVATING THE HOUSE

This chapter is not an attempt to tell you how to renovate or restore your house. Individual tastes and the distinct character of each city house make such a venture fruitless. The way in which you create your new environment is a matter best left to you and your architect. Instead I mean to give you some idea of what you will be facing when you set out to renovate a house, to point out some of the pitfalls, and to offer some suggestions that may make the task easier and more rewarding.

A surprisingly large number of houses available in urban centers require virtually no renovating at all. But such city houses are always expensive, and most houses available to you will require at least some minor renovation. Some will demand massive repairs, often rebuilding from the ground up. Usually the more renovation required, the lower the price of a city house.

Your architect can best guide you through the renovation process. A professional experienced in designing and redesigning environments, he can accurately evaluate the condition of your house and determine the kind and amount of work required. He can also save you considerable amounts of time and money. Other city homeowners, individuals who have already faced the problems of converting an old house into an environment for modern living, can supply both information and inspiration.

As I have mentioned before, writers of real estate ads frequently use three terms—"move in," "needs remodeling," and "shell"—to describe the condition of a city house. Although often misleading, these terms do describe the scope of the renovation job.

In the upper photograph, an entire brownstone facade is being refinished—an expensive undertaking. Such refinishing is often done badly, ruining the appearance of the house and affecting its resale value. The contractor should be chosen carefully, and you should examine other facades he has restored. Below, a great boon to the house renovator: a portable trash container that for a modest fee is left at your curb and taken away when full. These containers are available in various sizes. They fill up surprisingly fast—partly because of unsolicited contributions from housecleaning neighbors.

"MOVE IN"

"Move in" means basically what it says—that the house can be occupied immediately. In other words, the house will pass inspection by the city's building officials. It does not mean, however, that the house does not need work. In almost every case you will want to do at least some cosmetic renovation—painting, scraping and sanding floors, putting up wallpaper, etc. If cosmetic renovation is all the house needs I would advise moving in immediately, living in the house to get the "feel" of the structure, and renovating as you go along. If possible, do the work yourself. Contractors are expensive and in most cases you can do a better job yourself. Besides, that is part of the joy of owning a city house.

There are some instances, however, where you would be wise to put off occupying the house. The fact that such items as plumbing and wiring pass city inspections does not mean that they are in perfect condition. If the plumbing will have to be torn out and new plumbing installed in six months or a year, for example, you would be advised to have the work done at the outset. Ripping out plaster to get at old pipes is a messy job, one more easily and painlessly done when your house is not cluttered with furniture and children.

"NEEDS REMODELING"

"Needs remodeling" usually refers to a house where heavy renovation, such as structural changes or the tearing out of partitions, is necessary. Before you can begin work of this scope, plans must be filed with the city's building department. After the plans are approved and the work completed, the house must be inspected and a certificate of occupancy granted. Converting a rooming house to a one- or two-family dwelling would fall into this category, for example.

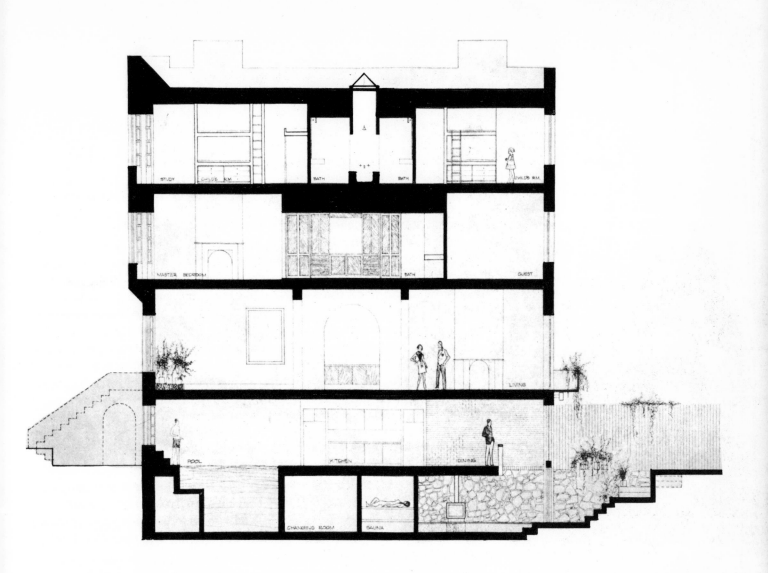

If you buy a one-family dwelling and wish to convert part of the house into apartments, you will also have to file plans with the building department. In most cities introducing only one apartment is a fairly simple procedure. For more than one apartment, however, the house becomes a multiple dwelling and sprinkler systems and fire escapes may have to be installed.One danger to watch for in a house that ''needs remodeling'' is the temptation (usually presented by an enterprising contractor) to ''gut it''—to rip out the insides of the house and start from the ground up. Although the house may seem beyond renovation, you should get expert advice before beginning the costly process of ''gutting.'' Often cleaning, painting, and minor repairs make more difference than you think they possibly could.

The section shows extensive remodeling in the basement and cellar, incorporating a two-level area and a swimming pool. The informal relationship of pool, kitchen, dining room, and garden is an excellent solution for a family with growing children. Other owners might have quite a different problem: providing an attractive entrance for a separate rental apartment. Below is a fine solution.

''SHELL''

The ''shell'' is a house with four walls and very little else. Until the recent surge of city-house restoration, shells were the sole province of the wrecker. They are now widely available and are, in most cases, the cheapest houses you can buy. Making a habitable structure out of a shell is, however, a large and expensive project.

An unprepossessing frame house in San Francisco has been transformed into a modern home without sacrificing its frame quality.

In mere renovating of city houses you are necessarily confined by the technology available when the house was built—in most cases the technology of the nineteenth century. Heated by fireplaces, rooms were necessarily small. Knocking down walls in these houses can open up space, but the possibilities are limited. With the shell, however, virtually the only confines are your imagination, your bank account, and the outside walls of your house. Renovation of a shell can result in a single room with a ceiling towering several stories above your head, or a maze of walkways and balconies opening onto rooms of all shapes and sizes, awesome skylights, walls of glass—the possibilities are endless.

If you set out to renovate a shell you should find a creative architect and do some serious thinking about how you will use the house. Here is a chance to create an environment exactly suited to your family. Carefully examine how you use the space you already have. What do you do in the kitchen besides cook and store food? Do you really use your living room? Flow charts of where traffic moves in the house or apartment you now live in can be very revealing. What rooms should join each other?

One questionable ambition when rebuilding a shell is to restore the house to its original appearance. It is an expensive process, and the result, no matter what the effort, is a new house made to look like an old one. If restoration is your intent, avoid buying a shell in the first place. Instead find a house with more complete details. It will cost more, but never as much as restoring a house with the help of present-day carpenters and painters.

DOING IT YOURSELF

Unless you are unusually skilled, any large renovation projects will require the services of a professional. Wiring and plumbing, even though you may think you can do them, must legally be done by licensed workmen. Such skilled labor is expensive, but necessary. Almost everything else, however, you can do yourself, if you have the time, the patience, the energy, and the desire.

Doing the work yourself will not only save you money. Usually it will result in a better job. The workmen you may hire, while they may have years of experience, will seldom be more careful with your property than you are. And some tedious, time-consuming jobs can become a surprisingly pleasant part of your evenings—spending an hour a day removing, stripping, and polishing brass hardware, or stripping dozens of yards of wainscotting, or scraping crusty paint from your front door can be relaxing after a day of paperwork, and each day a small but satisfying improvement is made.

Admittedly, you may know little or nothing about any kind of renovation work. But there are many books available on most renovation chores, and most of these tasks are not as complicated as they seem. Wallpapering, for example, is an enormously expensive operation if done by a contractor, yet it can be done at reasonable cost by the homeowner. Countless city homeowners have done handsome jobs in their own houses. Most of them now blanch at the thought of wallpaper paste, but they are proud of their accomplishment. And new types of wallpaper are now available at most hardware stores. Prepasted, these new

When it is necessary to paint a brick house, it helps to paint the trim in a contrasting color. Six-over-six and nine-over-nine windows lend interest to this facade.

wallpapers are simple to apply. Vinyl wallpaper, strong and easy to clean, is costly but desirable, and some new wallpapers are strippable—they can be easily removed without the aid of a steamer.

Stair carpeting is a task I can personally speak for. When I was renovating my own house I received estimates from several professional stair carpeters, and was staggered by the figures. I knew absolutely nothing about carpeting stairs but I thought that it couldn't be that difficult and plunged ahead. Working in the evenings, I carpeted a flight of stairs per day. At the last riser I found that I was out of carpeting and improvised a cut-and-fit technique that was perfectly satisfactory—in fact, quite professional.

One good way to educate yourself in a particular renovation task is to learn from a professional. If you decide to do your own plastering, hire a professional to plaster one room of your house, preferably a small one. While the plasterer is working you can watch him carefully, show a vague interest in his work, and ask questions. By the time he finishes you will have learned enough of his craft to tackle the rest of your house yourself. It will take some practice before you can lay on plaster with the casual ease of a professional—but you will be saving at least six dollars an hour, and when you are through you may well find that the room plastered by the professional is no better than, and perhaps not as good as, your own work.

Anyone can paint, especially with the rollers, sponge brushes, and quick-drying paints that are now common. Yet painters are expensive and will almost always do a poorer job than you could do yourself. If you do not want to take on the entire painting job, one way to save money is to have the painter do only the walls and ceiling, leaving the woodwork and trim. This is the time-consuming and therefore costly part of painting, and it is a task you can easily perform yourself.

The most tedious, costly, and in the long run most important part of painting is the preparation of the walls—filling holes with plaster or spackle, sanding, and removing old paint. Many professionals will skim over this part of the job, hurriedly get the paint on the walls, and call the job done. Then in a few months you begin to see chips and cracks. One city homeowner who tackled this job herself made an interesting discovery. Planning on perfectly smooth walls she decided to strip off the years of old paint with a blowtorch. (Small butane blowtorches are inexpensive and are excellent for stripping paint.) As she stripped one wall she noticed that the bare plaster, streaked with scorched paint of various muted shades, made an extremely attractive surface. Instead of repainting the walls of one room, she carefully painted the woodwork and ceiling and then applied a coat of clear varnish to the mottled plaster. She has solved the problem of flaking paint and added a unique and attractive feature to her house.

Refinishing wood floors, again an expensive job when done by professionals, is not difficult—although it is certainly hard, unpleasant work and generates a storm of dust. Floor sanders can be rented from many hardware stores for a small fee. The floors can then be stained or, in the case of the wide-board pine flooring found in many old houses, painted. For such pine flooring a mixture of white pigment and light opaque stain gives a rich butternut color. After the paint dries one of several durable varnishes, such as polyurethane, can be applied.

A house during and after facade renovation. The steel scaffolding can be rented. It is safer and more convenient than hanging scaffold and can be used for scraping, painting, and other processes the homeowner can do himself. Note that the parlor-floor windows have been lowered to their original position, a great improvement.

And larger, more hazardous jobs can be undertaken by the enterprising homeowner. More than a few energetic brownstoners have attacked non-load-bearing walls with a sledgehammer. Waffled tin ceilings, the rage in the 1890s, can be ripped out. Often they are covering intricate plasterwork in near-perfect condition. (This is definitely a gamble—the tin ceiling may have been installed to cover up plaster badly damaged by leakage. If this is the case the ceiling will have to be replastered, or the remaining plaster and lath ripped out to expose the beams.)

Unquestionably the best way to discover what renovation tasks you yourself can undertake is to consult an expert—another city homeowner who has been through the adventure of renovating a house. He will probably suggest you go ahead with the job, and then pitch in and help you do it.

HIRING HELP

Hiring electricians, plumbers, plasterers, and other workmen can be a dismal business. Stories of shoddy workmanship, workmen not showing up for months, astounding errors, and extra charges lumped onto the original price of the job are the brownstoners' cocktail conversation. Yet there is little you can do to avoid these problems, especially for small jobs. You can ask for references, but often it is the self-employed man, recently emigrated and without references, who will do the best work for the lowest price. It is a good idea to ask other city-house owners if they know workmen who could suit your needs. If your electrician is good, ask him to recommend a plumber, who, in turn, may suggest a plasterer. Publications for city homeowners, such as *The Brownstoner* in New York, advertise workmen, and you can be fairly sure that these men at least have had some experience with the problems of the city house and are interested in working for you.

CONTRACTORS

If you hire individual workmen, you can afford to take a chance on how they will work out, but you should be considerably more cautious when hiring a contractor to handle the renovation of your house. A great deal more money is involved and the problems are graver. First, demand references from every contractor you consider employing. And then check the references out. References alone, however, are not signs that you will get good work—no contractor would refer you to a client he has left unsatisfied. But the references will let you know that the contractor has at least done acceptable work for somebody.

You should then check the contractor's reputation with such organizations as the Better Business Bureau, NERSICA (the National Established Repair, Service, and Improvement Contractors Association), and the National Association of Home Builders. From these groups you can discover whether complaints have been made against the contractor.

Once you are satisfied with a contractor's reputation you should then ask for bids on the project. It is commonly thought that you can lower the bid by letting

121

Only a specialized mason can restore the stone-work at left. Renovating of the stoops should include replacing the masonry walls with iron railing.

the contractor know that you intend to get as many bids as possible before selecting your man. In fact it is often the other way around. Careful estimates cost a contractor time, and if he thinks you are not serious about hiring him he will make a rough estimate and necessarily come up with a *higher* figure. If, however, the contractor suspects he has a good chance of winding up with the job he will be inclined to spend the time to study your situation carefully and come up with a good estimate. Some reputable contractors figure that, given enough assurance to warrant a careful estimate, they can lower the price of a job by as much as 20 percent.

Once you have selected a contractor, the best way to be sure you will receive your money's worth is to enter into a good contract. First of all the contract should describe the work to be done in careful detail. Here a good architect is invaluable to draw up exact plans and specifications. These plans and specifications should be included as the subject matter of the contract.

A New York lawyer knowledgeable in this area has suggested that the following terms should be stated in the contract in addition to the work specifications:

1. The price to be paid.
2. When payment is to be made and in what installments (usually as the work progresses).
3. The number of days after work is started within which all of the work is to be completed.
4. Penalties for failure to complete work within the time agreed, and a bonus for completion earlier than scheduled.
5. A provision for furnishing a certificate showing that Workmen's Compensation insurance is in full force and effect.
6. A provision that a city building inspection certificate accepting the work must be obtained before final payment.
7. Warranties and guarantees of materials and workmanship and the period of time within which the mechanic will redo any faulty work and replace any faulty materials. Also, specify that the mechanic exhibit paid bills for all appliances and merchandise delivered on the job before being entitled to final payment.

New iron railing replacing masonry walls opens the basement to light and air and in this case is a pleasant contrast to the heavy stone facade.

NEW TECHNOLOGY AND MATERIALS

Unfortunately, most of today's city houses are designed for looking, or photographing, but seldom for living. We now live in an age when rockets put men on the moon, yet the technology in our houses is only slightly more advanced than in our parents' houses, or our grandparents' houses, for that matter. Look at your stove, for example. Unless you have an unusual appliance or are over seven feet tall, the burners on your stove are probably six inches too high. Put a saucepan full of water on your stove, reach for the handle, and see the awkward position you must assume.

Thankfully, architects, designers, and manufacturers are finally considering people in their designs and products, and breakthroughs in home technology are beginning to be made. There are many new materials, easy to use and maintenance-free. To cite one example, metal tile, weighing only 3½ pounds per square foot, is now available. The tile is easily installed on a grooved foundation sheet that ensures automatic tile alignment. You (not an expensive tile-setter) can cover the walls of an average bathroom in a day, and the room will weigh a ton less than if finished with clay tile. You should be aware of all these advances as they occur—like many homeowners, you may become a regular reader of the various consumer magazines that report on home technology. In the next few years some incredible things will find their way into the city house. One you can definitely expect is the computer, right next to your television and stereo.

Two adjacent houses can be transformed into luxurious floor-throughs, as shown in the plan below. The apartment is nearly 2000 sq. ft.

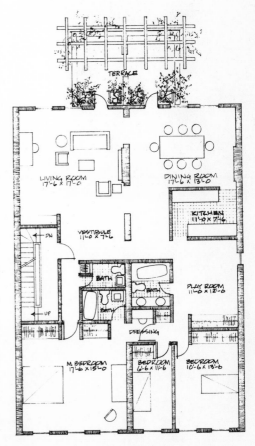

123

The owners of the Greenwich Village brownstone pictured here live in the top two floors of their house, an area of only 1200 square feet. The renovation made practical use of such existing features as skylights and fireplaces. Since many of the walls were in poor repair, shelves and cabinets were added to hide unsightly spots and simplify room shapes. Structural changes were minimal.

This house in lower Manhattan is only twelve feet wide, but interpenetrating spaces, sometimes including three floors, give it an open feeling. Old surfaces and shapes, such as the railing salvaged from another building, are used very successfully. The house is an excellent example of what can be done with a shell.

SIX | SOME CITY HOUSES

Of the four houses discussed in the text of this chapter, two were bought and renovated with relative ease; two were beset with extreme problems. To protect the owners' privacy I have used fictitious names. One of the easy ones and one of the difficult ones are illustrated in some detail, and there are also picture stories of several other houses.

THE DIFFICULTIES OF URBAN RENEWAL

Peter Sergeant bought a three-story brick row house in one of New York's urban-renewal areas. He was well aware of the advantages of moving into the area, the most obvious being an FHA mortgage at 3 percent with some tax abatements and exemptions. After he purchased the house he began to experience the disadvantages.

The renovation required was considerable. To convert from a rooming house to a two-family dwelling a new kitchen had to be added on the stoop floor. The existing kitchen on the basement floor, to be used to service the garden apartment, was inadequate and had to be replaced. The house had to be completely rewired and new plumbing was needed.

Under the terms of the urban-renewal program Sergeant was to be supplied architect's plans for the renovation—drawn to meet the standards and goals of the area—and a work order, a detailed written description of the work required. Here Sergeant experienced the first of many delays. He contacted the urban-

renewal office almost daily, but the plans were months in coming. When he finally received the plans and work order he was told to employ his own contractor. Under the terms of the FHA mortgage, however, he was given a limit on the amount he could spend on the renovation required by the program. Sergeant contacted several contractors and received bids. Only one bid fell within the set limit, and he was forced to use this contractor, who was recommended by the renewal agency representative.

The contractor immediately had problems with the plans and specifications. The plans were poorly drawn and virtually unreadable. Sergeant later discovered that the architect responsible had never actually seen the house. The work order had been written by an inexperienced official of the urban-renewal board. The descriptions were vague, and quality and size designations were not specific, resulting in additional costs.

The work finally began and seemed to be progressing for about a month. Then there was a two-month period during which no workmen appeared at the house. Finally most of the work was completed, the certificate of occupancy was issued, and Sergeant moved in.

The disappointments were many, however. The new walls and corners were out of plumb. All electric light fixtures rose out of bulges in the plaster. Plaster moldings were broken and not replaced. Doorways were located in partitions with no allowance for door jambs and the surround of wood trim. In short, the workmanship was a nightmare and there was no adequate recourse through the controlling agency. The contractor had borrowed to the hilt against his payments so that when they came due, his creditors collected all but a small percentage of the payment. This resulted in several impasses during which the contractor would disappear, returning only on the promise of payments. Finally, at the first feasible opportunity, Sergeant fired the contractor, hired his own carpenter and painter, and finished the work.

Once firmly entrenched in his new house, Sergeant weighed the advantages of the urban-renewal program against the disadvantages. Even considering that he had lost more than half a year's rent in delays, he discovered that the low interest rate and the tax benefits over-balanced most of the disadvantages, at least financially. But no such benefits can compensate him for the damage done to his house. It would be too costly to try to make it a creditable job now.

AN OBVIOUS SOLUTION TO URBAN-RENEWAL PROBLEMS

Mr. and Mrs. Neil Von Daniken purchased their house in an urban-renewal area in August 1968, began massive renovation around Christmas, and moved into the house the following October. The renovation was beautifully executed, and carried out virtually without a hitch. They employed a simple tactic: they ignored the benefits of urban renewal and financed the house independently of the program, through a bank. Their interest rate was high and there were no tax benefits, but they avoided the usual headaches.

A stairway curve or angle occurs in almost every row house and is a difficult area to repair or renovate. Here the combined curves of molding, wainscot, banister, and stair stringer are in harmony.

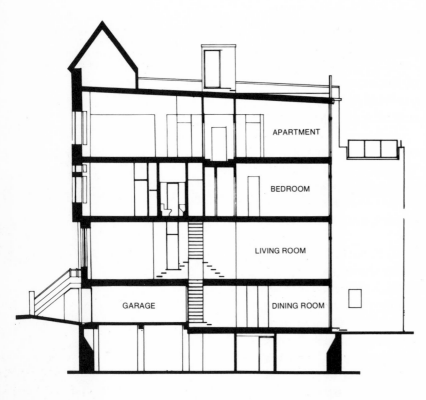

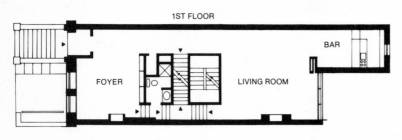

1ST FLOOR

FOYER

LIVING ROOM

BAR

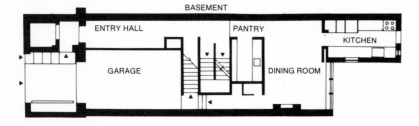

BASEMENT

ENTRY HALL

PANTRY

KITCHEN

GARAGE

DINING ROOM

This is the Von Daniken house, which is described in the text. Note the spiral staircase from the living room down to the garden. The kitchen and pantry are separated by the dining room. In the plan this appears inconvenient, but it is actually quite practical, because the isolated pantry provides protection for the owners' collection of antique dinnerware.

The house was a vacant, rundown rooming house. The Von Danikens had the house completely gutted and rebuilt from scratch. The only original materials kept in the house were the four exterior walls, the front doors, and the paneling in the "Victorian bar." Perhaps the most interesting feature of the renovation was the inclusion of an enclosed, central-core staircase to serve the tenants who occupied the top floor. This staircase, which replaced a broken-down, ugly, Victorian staircase, allows the Von Danikens and their tenants to use the full 19-foot width of the house in all major rooms.

Unusual for a brownstone with a north garden, the house now has a four-story glass wall in the rear. It also has a one-car private garage on the ground floor, complete with heating pad in the garage ramp for bad weather. It is my own feeling that enclosing a garage in your brownstone is an expensive luxury indeed. It is certainly convenient, and your car will not suffer so much at the hands of garage attendants. But consider that the space taken up by the car is about the same as that taken up by a small efficiency apartment. Car storage is expensive, but the day is still far off that it will be as expensive as a new apartment.

A HOUSE IN MOVE-IN CONDITION

John and Carol Alderson wanted a house in good condition. They could afford the cost and meant to move in as soon as possible. The house they found was a 21-foot-wide Italianate brownstone that had been occupied by the same family ever since it had been built a century before. The family sold the Aldersons the house furnished, complete with glassware, dishes, and silver.

The Aldersons' architect carefully went through their new possessions, suggesting things they should keep. There were several valuable antiques and some furniture that could be restored. The architect also suggested they keep such things as towels, useful as rags for cleaning and refinishing during the renovation process.

They liked the wide, gently graded staircase, but it prompted the only major renovation work. Because of this staircase the Aldersons decided to put the kitchen on the second floor, using what is usually the master bedroom for a dining room. Such a design requires carrying groceries up two flights and garbage down two flights, but the comfortable stairs led them to accept this inconvenience.

The rest of the work was merely cosmetic. On the stoop floor are two large living rooms, divided by etched-glass sliding doors. All the woodwork in these rooms was pine, painted maroon and grained. The Aldersons had the woodwork repainted. Marble fireplaces, also painted maroon, were stripped to a gleaming white. Wall-to-wall carpeting had been installed in the living room when the building was originally built. This has been replaced with white vinyl flooring and area rugs. The original woodwork, painted with a dark reddish stain to resemble dark mahogany, has been retained, with navy-blue walls offsetting the giltwork of the mirror and drapery moldings.

Perhaps the outstanding feature of this house was the beautifully preserved ornate plasterwork. Garlands of flowers, painted in pastels, circle the center ceiling canopy in the main living room. These have been retained wherever possible. Plasterwork garlands applied to the original wallpaper were carefully left when the wallpaper was removed. The effect is stunning, not unlike the original but with a very contemporary feeling, mostly because of the combination of blue walls, old woodwork, and white and gold accessories.

THE HARDSHIPS OF RENOVATION

In 1967, tired of apartment living, Bill and Elizabeth Graham began to search for a city house. They looked at dozens of row houses, and learned a great deal from the looking. One house, a handsome brownstone in almost perfect condition, going for a bargain price, they remember painfully. They rejected the house solely because of a particularly unattractive school of angel fish painted on the tiles in the master bathroom.

Finally, in June of 1967, the Grahams purchased a four-story brick house on a block in Manhattan where considerable renovation was already under way. The house, built in 1875, had a distinct Mediterranean flavor, with an impressive Moorish arch extending across the front. The price was $25,000. Broken up into eight apartments, the house still had two tenants firmly entrenched when the purchase was made.

Faced with a considerable renovation job, the Grahams began looking for an architect. (During this time they also persuaded the two remaining tenants to move out—persuasion that amounted to several thousand dollars.) They had definite ideas about design, and interviewed a number of architects, often inspecting other row houses the architects had renovated. Late in July they found an architect whose work they admired and whose ideas were compatible with their own, and they awarded him the job.

In the fall, after what seemed an interminable time, the architect's plans were completed to the Grahams' satisfaction, submitted to the city's Building Department, and approved. They were now ready to hire a contractor and begin renovation.

They had estimated that the renovation would cost somewhere in the vicinity of $40,000. But when bids from contractors were submitted, the lowest bid was $62,000, and the highest was nearly $100,000. After some deliberation, the Grahams accepted the $62,000 bid and awarded the contract. Then, in March of 1968, the nightmare began.

The renovation was scheduled to be completed in September of 1968, and the Grahams imagined that all they had left to do was make their payments to the contractor and wait. They were not to be so lucky.

By the third payment they noticed that the work completed did not match the money spent. The contractor, they were later to discover, was using their money to pay for materials and labor on other jobs. By June of 1968—four months after the contract had been awarded, and three months from the completion date—

The Grahams' house. Unrestorable masonry has been replaced by delicate ironwork stairs. The upper facade, which originally attracted them into the house, has not been disturbed.

there was no rough plumbing in the house. The Grahams complained, but still the work progressed at snail's pace. By December of 1968, three months past the completion date, the rough plumbing was still not installed.

As the completion date slipped further into history, the contractor became more and more difficult to reach. Phone calls found him unfortunately out of the office, and messages left were unanswered. Finally, after a host of letters and calls, the contractor was located and a meeting arranged.

In the parlor of their house, amid piles of rubble and miscellaneous pieces of the still-to-be-installed plumbing, the contractor claimed he would have to have an advance to complete the work. The Grahams, by now desperate to get the work finished, threw caution out their front window, and wrote out a check.

Six months after the scheduled date of completion, there was still no running water in the house. Part of the plumbing had indeed been installed, but inspection of this turned up more than forty leaks. After paying more than $45,000 the Grahams were at the end of their patience. In March of 1969, they fired the contractor.

Firing a contractor is virtually unheard-of. The contractor immediately filed suit against the Grahams. They, in turn, sued the contractor, sparking a complicated legal battle that is still to be settled.

Most couples would have admitted defeat long before. The Grahams, in fact, seriously considered selling the house. They would have to take a heavy loss, but at least the nightmare would be over. Gazing at that fine Moorish arch, however, they decided that they couldn't part with the house. Sitting on boxes in what was envisioned as their living room, they made plans: Elizabeth would become the contractor, and Bill would be her job foreman. That is, Elizabeth would set about telephoning for missing materials and trying to locate workmen to assist as plumbers, electricians, or just plain laborers, while Bill would instruct the workmen in each phase of the work in order to establish a proper sequence of events, making certain that the various segments of the work would be finished before the next workman arrived on the scene.

A few days later, clad in dungarees and a sweat shirt, tape measure in hand, Elizabeth watched the plumbers she had hired finish one phase of their work. A plasterer who had worked on the house earlier—and who had not been paid by the contractor—stopped by, and Elizabeth put him to work. She discovered that one of her neighbors was a carpenter, and when she saw the work he had done on his own house, she hired him. The architect himself pitched in. The renovation was finally under way.

In July of 1969 the Grahams moved out of their apartment and into the house. At this writing, the renovation is nearly completed. The problems they faced were extreme, but they believe the results are worth the effort. They found that they genuinely enjoyed doing much of the work themselves. They are now seriously considering buying and restoring another house in the same neighborhood. If they do, Elizabeth will be the contractor, and Bill will be the foreman.

The special feature of the Grahams' house is the huge central skylight. The lighting effect is extremely pleasant, and many people are reminded of an atrium-style Renaissance palazzo. The view in the photograph is from the top floor looking down to the music room and the dining area.

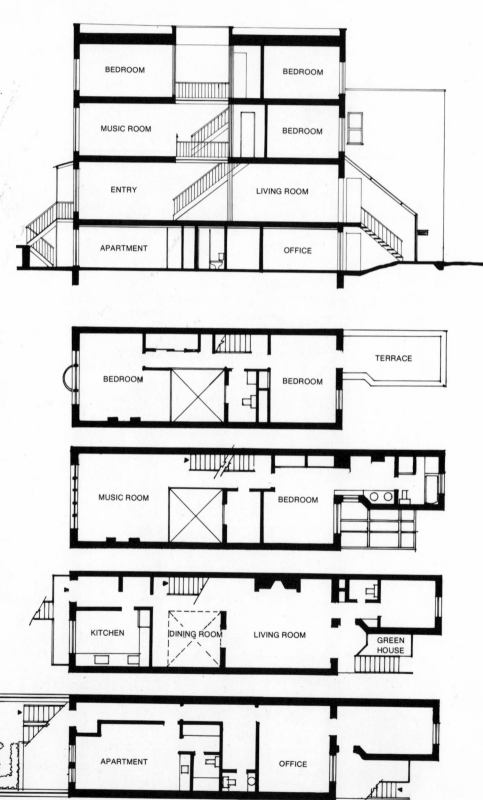

The Grahams preserved the purity of their arched window on the inside as well as on the outside. There are interior windows opening onto the light well. The small lean-to greenhouse at the back of the living room incorporates a staircase leading down to the office.

Another handsome house. The sensitively remodeled ornate exterior has been achieved by replacing double-hung sash with single-pane pivoting sash and adding vertical louvered blinds.

The owner's apartment is on the top floor and utilizes a terrace as part of the living room. Again, a clerestory in the kitchen area provides light and air in the center of the building.

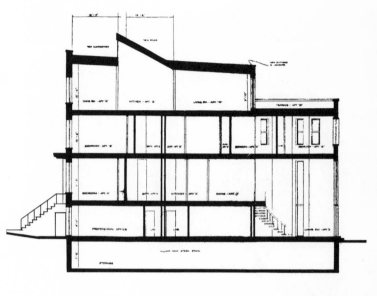

In renovating this house, no changes were made in the facade, but the lower two floors of the rear wall were completely redesigned, and the extensive interior remodeling took several years of painstaking detail work. In the south-facing garden a free-standing wood pergola rises on a platform above a gravel area. The living room is the full width of the house and looks out on the garden. The dining room is lined with grasscloth panels.

More of the same house. An almost Japanese simplicity permeates the interiors. The ground-floor garden room, which the owner, an architect, uses as his office, is a study in planes of salmon-colored brick. Elsewhere almost all surfaces are smooth. The bedrooms have been given an intimate scale by raised fireplaces, rosewood wardrobes that do not reach the ceiling, and indirect lighting. The house shows extremely careful attention to detail; note the artful arrangement of stones and firewood on the raised hearth of one of the bedroom fireplaces. The kitchen is compact, with under-counter refrigerator and dishwasher, but makes a handsome display of cooking utensils. The bathrooms are lighted through an overhead plastic ceiling.

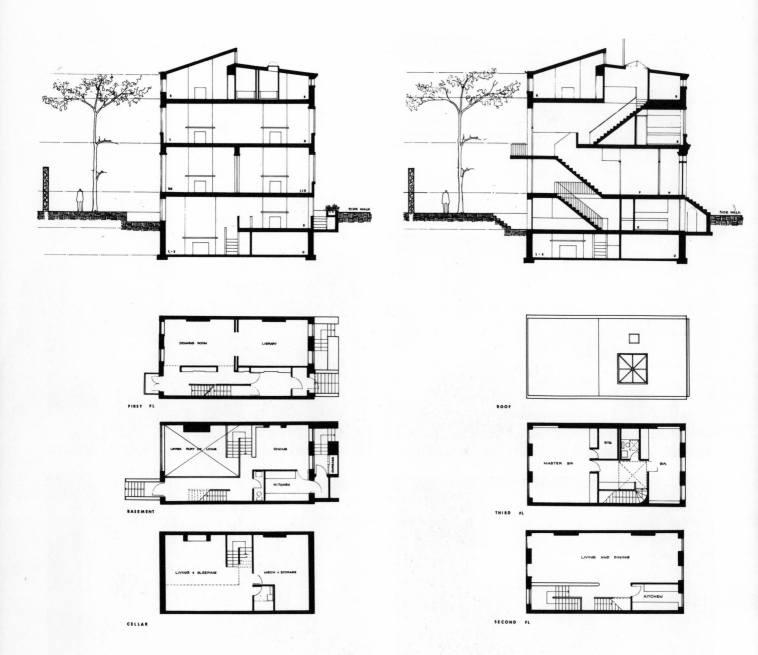

SIDE WALK

FIRST FL

DRAWING ROOM   LIBRARY

BASEMENT

UPPER PART OF LIVING   DINING

KITCHEN

CELLAR

LIVING & SLEEPING   MECH & STORAGE

SIDE WALK

ROOF

THIRD FL

MASTER BR   BR

SECOND FL

LIVING AND DINING

KITCHEN

A renovation in progress in Greenwich Village. The Greek Revival house has survived much misuse. The sills of the front windows at the stoop level were originally at the level of the stone base. Note the small windows in the entablature. The rear view shows the new stairhall window. The sections and plans show most dramatically the new volumes that are being created. The two duplex apartments each have variety, style, and a two-story openness; opening the basement and cellar at the rear of the house was important in achieving this effect.

As often in gutted houses, the old stone and brick become part of the new design. In the cellar room, a clerestory provides natural light and the massive raised hearth echoes the foundation wall. The photographs on this page show both levels of the upper duplex, looking toward the back of the house.

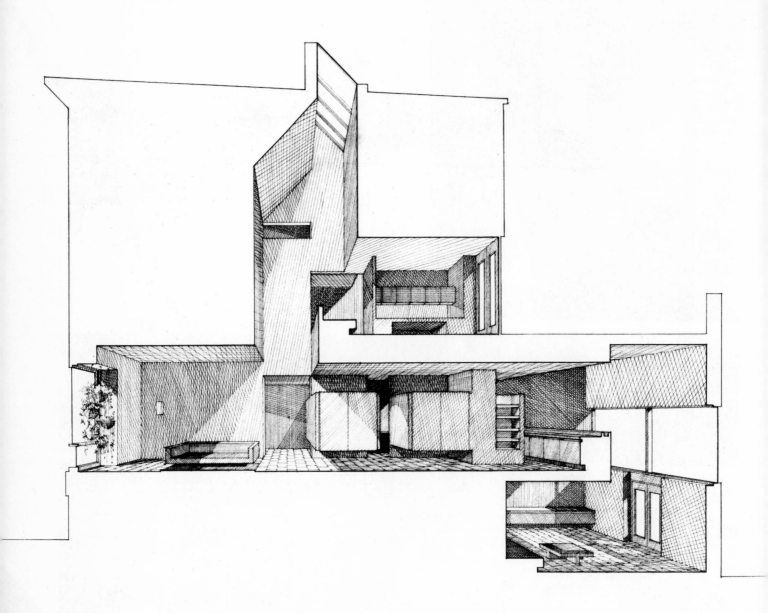

An extensively remodeled house in Brooklyn Heights, owned by a husband-and-wife architect team. The simplified perspective section shows the main living areas of the house. A skylight illuminates the areas usually dark in a row house. The main living-dining area is a floor-through, and the kitchen overlooks a two-story playroom and the garden. The middle level is the architects' work area. The small window in the top of the light well is in the stair hall.

More of the architects' house. The photograph below shows the street entrance at the extreme right, leading up to the living floor. The large photograph at left is the view of the architects' work area from the light-well window.

APPENDIX

SEQUENCE OF PROCEDURES FOR TYPICAL RENOVATION

It is inevitable in almost any renovation project that there will be some wasted effort and duplicated effort. Especially if you are doing much of the work yourself, you are often tempted to take on projects in the wrong order. For example, you may decide, on first taking possession of your house, that the most important thing is to repaint a room or two to make it livable so that you can move in. That may indeed be the practical thing to do, if it means you can stop paying rent sooner. However, you are apt to find after you have painted the room that you really should have repaired some of the plaster first. So you begin breaking away the worst plaster, hoping you will be able to patch the holes and touch up without too much trouble. But you find there are quite large sections that need complete replastering. You do this, and are quite pleased with the fine smooth appearance of the redone sections—in fact, they make the older sections look a little shabby, but...well, you can live with it. Then you paint the new sections, and discover that it is very difficult to match paint on the fresh plaster surface with the rest of the room. Perhaps you should have primed the new plaster in some way—but it is too late now. Anyway, a final coat over the whole room makes the borders between new and old sections quite inconspicuous, and you are satisfied. The room looks fine, and as soon as a few more electrical outlets are installed it will be finished. The electrician has just begun to rewire, and you explain that you want this room done first so that you can begin living in it. You watch him work his way around the room with a heavy screwdriver, making holes through to the lath every foot or so, through old and new plaster alike, so that he can get his cables into the walls...

If you have a general contractor, you will not make that sort of mistake, but you can make much bigger ones: you can change your mind about what needs doing. If you have new hardwood floors put down, sanded, and finished and then decide to remove a partition wall, the floor will have to be patched together, probably not very satisfactorily. Perhaps there is new wiring and plumbing in the wall, too—so you either spend a great deal of money redoing work or you resign yourself to keeping the partition wall, which would have been so easy to remove a few months before.

An architect can help you avoid the big mistakes, too, because he not only knows what the proper sequence of procedures should be but also studies the house, your needs, and you yourself and helps you make decisions you will be happy with and will not want to change. Removing a partition wall might not occur to you until it is too late, but an architect would very likely mention the possibility, among many others, on his first visit to the house. If you decide to have it removed, it is done as part of an orderly demolition program, and the plumbing and wiring may even be slightly cheaper to install, because the plumber and electrician do not have to cope with finished walls.

This is not to say that everyone who buys a row house should have a rigid plan and stick to it. Renovating a house is a creative process, and it may take months or even years of living in a house before you are aware of its possibilities. There may be wasted effort. One couple bought their house several years ago, at a very good price, and lived in it for two years, patching up room after room, spending almost all their free time painting or removing paint, plastering or removing plaster. Their house became clean and comfortable for the most part, though it was still basically a fixed-up ex-roominghouse and showed it. In the meantime, they saw many

renovated houses, other young couples began working on houses in their own neighborhood, they began to be more aware of the possibilities of their house, they became more ambitious—and, happily, their income increased considerably. They hired an architect and a general contractor and did a real job. Walls they had plastered and painted, staircases they had braced, even floors they had sanded and finished went out the door in pieces and were trucked away. Yet much of their labor—the handsome entryway woodwork they had stripped, the brickwork they had exposed, the rafters they had exposed, sanded, and stained—was not wasted. Moreover, all their work, wasted or not, had been an education to them: they had learned to understand their house and what they wanted from it, and when they finally did call in the architect and contractor they were able to plan and build a home that will please them for many years to come.

Nevertheless, there are more efficient and less efficient ways of re-modeling a house. Outlined below is a list of the significant stages, in the order that will most avoid wasted effort. *Nothing* should be done, of course, until after the closing, when the property becomes yours.

1. *Check security of the property.* This is important even if the building is vacant and there seems to be nothing inside to steal. Even plumbing and waste pipes are frequently torn out, and the lead and brass sold to junk dealers for perhaps one-hundredth of what it will cost to replace the plumbing. A vandal might smash a marble mantel, swing on a chandelier, break a pierglass. You should consciously try to figure out ways of breaking in, and then take temporary or permanent measures to discourage a thief. If the building is in first-class move-in condition, with plenty of iron gates and bars, window locks, and door locks, you still should have a locksmith change all the locks. More typically, you will be able to find gaps in the security system. There are many ways into a row house: usually a cellar window in front and one in back; two front doors and a rear door; windows, often within easy reach from adjoining sheds, fire escapes, etc.; and roof skylights, at least one of which is probably designed to open for roof access. Use wire netting, planks, padlocks and chains, nails—anything to protect the weak points.

2. *Clean up.* If the house has been left in a mess, with old clothes, broken furniture, newspapers, mattresses, and so on in every room, clean it out. This will improve the outlook, and as you clean you will make some discoveries about the house, some bad (roaches everywhere), some good (parquet floors under the linoleum, even on the top floors).

3. *Study demolition.* Investigate walls, ceilings, floors, and staircases to determine what *must* go. Try to decide what additional demolition you will want. Note: Unless you are gutting the building, demolition should be done not by a demolition contractor but by a carpenter, preferably the one who will be doing the renovation. He will do a neater job and will salvage whatever he can.

4. *Carry out demolition.* Even if you do not plan much demolition, it is better to try to do it all at once at an early stage, not just for the reasons given above but also because it is very messy. A partition wall only a few feet long quickly becomes many bushels of plaster fragments and broken lath—no problem if you have rented a trash container (see the photograph on page 116), but a great problem if you are doing the demolition gradually and trying to smuggle the trash out a little at a time in the garbage. After the demolition, you will, of course, have to clean the house again, and probably vacuum for several days running until all the dust has settled.

During the demolition, be sure to protect any floors you plan to keep; if there is linoleum on them, leave it there for the time being.

5. *Replace windows if necessary.* Unless you are planning to change the shape of window openings, inspect all window sash and sills and replace those that are rotted, warped, or broken. Your architect, contractor, or carpenter can help you decide if a window needs replacing or just scraping and painting and reputtying. (Window sash is not expensive, and it is often worth replacing it even if it is sound, if it is covered with many coats of lumpy paint.)

6. *Have rough plumbing installed.* Supply pipes, waste pipes and vents, and heating pipes should all be installed and tested before any open walls are closed.

7. *Have wiring completed.* Work out a detailed plan, with your architect if you have one, of where you want every fixture, every outlet, and every switch. The new wiring should be inspected and in use before any plastering is done.

8. *Build new partitions.* Usually partitions are simple 2 x 4 framing. Interior walls of closets can be finished at this time with plasterboard, which is easier and cheaper to use than plaster.

9. *Install bathroom and kitchen fixtures.* Bathroom tilework can be done at this point too, since all plumbing and wiring is roughed in.

10. *Plaster.* Walls and ceilings are best finished with rock lath or wire lath and three coats of plaster. All the holes left by the demolition, plumbing, and wiring can be filled. This is one of the most dramatic and satisfying stages of renovation; interior spaces suddenly take on shape as the plaster hardens to a fine true plane. The plaster should cure for two weeks before it is painted.

11. *Finish carpentry.* Install door trim, hang doors, etc. Interior hardware such as doorknobs can be installed, but escutcheons around knobs will have to be removed later while painting.

12. *Install electric fixtures.* Overhead lights, chandeliers, wall sconces, track lights, etc. should be installed before painting since additional plaster patching may be necessary.

13. *Paint.* Another dramatic moment. Hardware, electric fixtures, and outlet and switch plates should be temporarily removed for a neat job.

14. *Finish floors.* Lay new floors, or scrape and sand the old ones. It is usually easier just to paint floors of narrow (four-inch) pine planking rather than sand them. But wide-board floors are worth the trouble of sanding, and the four-inch floors have a pleasant antiqued look if some of the old paint is left in the crevices.

PRICES OF SURFACING MATERIALS

The new homeowner has little difficulty understanding the plumbing contractor who tells hims a new tub will cost $100 and a new sink $50—the article itself is worth part of that sum, and the labor of installing it is obvious.

He also has no difficulty computing the cost of wallpapering a room, if he is going to do the job himself. But he often feels at the mercy of the contractor when he is quoted a price that includes a considerable labor charge, as for plastering a ceiling. The prices given below are fair ones at the time of writing. The price range is from nonunion "handyman" labor to union-scale expert labor, and the surfacing materials are standard, not custom or luxury. Prices are per square foot.

Walls

Gypsum board ready for painting	.20- .26
Painting	.06- .16
Paper to vinyl wall covering	.08-1.00
Plaster, 3 coats, any surface	.30- .50
Ceramic tile	2.25-2.75

Floors

Hardwood	.60-1.00
Refinish old floor	- .30
Vinyl asbestos tile	.37- .45
Vinyl tile	.52- .63
Carpeting	.55-1.65
Seamless mastic paving	- .90
Ceramic tile	1.75-2.25
Quarry tile	1.85-2.25

Ceilings

Gypsum board	.25- .30
Plaster, 3 coats over metal lath	.55- .85
Painting	.09- .18

It is quite easy, if occasionally discouraging, to use these figures to estimate the cost of a project you have in mind. Suppose you would like to do a thorough job on your back parlor. It measures fifteen by twenty feet and has a twelve-foot ceiling. You want a new hardwood floor, a tricky job because of the fireplace, alcoves, and closets. The wall plaster is in fair shape, but has been painted many times before, and rather than repaint it you want to cover it with a good grade of wallpaper that you estimate will cost about 30¢ a square foot installed. The ceiling must come down; the history of the house includes a series of disasters in the bathroom above. The plaster molding is miraculously undamaged all the way around the room, however, so you decide to get the best job done you can. A few minutes with paper and pencil and you will know what it all should cost:

Floor: 300 square feet x $1.00	$300.00
Walls: 680 square feet x $0.30 (12 x 15 + 12 x 15 + 12 x 20 + 12 x 20 = 840, less 160 square feet for doors and windows)	204.00
Ceiling: 300 square feet x $0.85	255.00
	$759.00

Too much? Well, you can achieve most of the effect you want, and save $300, by just doing the ceiling and walls and putting the floor off for a year or so. Or you can try refinishing the present floor, which will cost only $90.

RECOMMENDED BOOKS

General and Sociological

Lowe, Jeanne R. *Cities in a Race with Time.* New York: Random House.

Lyford, Joseph P. *The Airtight Cage: A Study of New York's West Side.* New York: Harper, Colophon Books.

Lynch, Kevin. *The Image of the City.* Cambridge: M.I.T.

Tauber, Gilbert, and Samuel Kaplan. *The New York City Handbook.* New York: Doubleday.

Home Buying and Improvement

Edgerton, William H., et al. *How to Renovate a Brownstone.* New York: Halsey, 1970.

Hornung, William J. *Reinhold Data Sheets.* New York: Van Nostrand Reinhold, 1965.

Huff, Darrell. *Complete Book of Home Improvement.* New York: Harper, 1970.

Moger, Byron J., and Burke. *How to Buy a House.* New York: Lyle Stuart, 1969.

Schuler, Stanley. *Home Building and Remodeling.* New York: Macmillan.

Watkins, Arthur M. *How to Avoid the 10 Biggest Home-Buying Traps.* New York: Meredith.

Home Buyer's Guide to New York City Brownstone Neighborhoods. Brownstone Revival Committee, 230 Park Avenue, New York, N.Y. 10017.

The Brownstoner. Publication of the Brownstone Revival Committee.

Wine Cellars. Wine Institute, 717 Market Street, San Francisco, Calif.

Historical and Architectural

Delaney, Edmond T. *New York's Turtle Bay, Old and New.* Barre, 1965.

Dober, Richard. *Environmental Design.* New York: Van Nostrand Reinhold, 1969.

Eastlake, Charles L. *Hints on Household Taste.* New York: Dover.

Huxtable, Ada L. *Classic New York: Georgian Gentility to Greek Elegance.* New York: Doubleday.

Kennedy, Robert Woods. *The House and the Art of Its Design.* New York: Van Nostrand Reinhold, 1953.

Lancaster, Clay. *Old Brooklyn Heights.* Rutland, Vt.: Tuttle, 1961.

Silver, Nathan. *Lost New York.* Boston: Houghton-Mifflin, 1967.

Smithson, Alison and Peter. *Urban Structuring.* New York: Van Nostrand Reinhold, 1967.

White, Norval, and Elliott Willensky. *AIA Guide to New York City.* New York: Macmillan, 1968.

Legal

Pyke, J. *Landmark Preservation.* Citizen's Union Research.

Tomson, Bernard, and Norman Coplan. *Architectural and Engineering Law.* New York: Van Nostrand Reinhold, 1967.

Walker, N., et al. *Legal Pitfalls in Architecture, Engineering, and Building Construction.* New York: McGraw-Hill, 1968.